Praise for Lucas Mann's

LORD FEAR

"Lucas Mann's genre-bending first book, *Class A* . . . heralded an impressive new talent in narrative nonfiction. Mann's second book, *Lord Fear*, reaffirms that talent . . . [and] demonstrates that Mann is a writer who avoids reductionism, instead embracing complexity and uncertainty."

—Heller McAlpin, NPR

"I read this book in a sustained state of near-tears. . . . *Lord Fear* is the most evocative treatment of this kind of crooked adolescent male logic that I've ever read, and the most affecting elicitation of boys' conflicted thirst for danger. . . . I read it with gratitude." —John Lingan, *Chicago Tribune*

"[T]his exquisite tension of knowing and not knowing . . . lends the book its power and makes it worth sinking your teeth into." —*Esquire*

"Both moving and intimate. . . . It's rare to find a book that reads as if it were written out of necessity. This book is one; absorbing and with an undeniable current of truth."

—Oprah.com

"In constructing his aching, poignant narrative, Mann offers a fine meditation on fate and on how 'the story of addiction is the story of memory, and how we never get it right.'"

—*Kirkus Reviews* (starred review)

"Mann creates a stunning, and chilling, portrait."

—*Los Angeles Review of Books*

"In *Lord Fear*, Mann folds Josh's writings in with contemplative renderings of his interviews, imbuing those conversations with the buzz and herky-jerky flow of a postmodern detective novel. The result is a nonlinear, scrapbook-style investigative memoir as redolent of the bluesy crime pursuits of Raymond Chandler's Philip Marlowe as it is of the narcotized reveries of William Burroughs." —*San Francisco Chronicle*

"This is an awesome, emotionally riveting memoir."

—*Providence Journal*

"[D]elicately rendered and hyper–self aware; with this unflinching, fractured examination of his brother, Mann suggests that writing about and investigating any life produces infinite contradictory representations that orbit around an indefinable center. Mann is driving at how we know that unknowable thing—taking us right up to language's edge, where we watch him peer over." —*Paris Review*

"This is a moving, frightening, expertly written book that stands at the nexus of imagination, encounter, document, and dirge." —Maggie Nelson, author of *The Art of Cruelty*

"Mann has a knack for tracking down uncomfortahle truths . . . and burrowing in, like a metaphysical gumshoe, where others would turn away. [He] wants us to know his beautiful mess of a brother better than he ever did." —*New York*

Lucas Mann
LORD FEAR

Lucas Mann was born in New York City and received his MFA from the University of Iowa, where he was the Provost's Visiting Writer in Nonfiction. He is the author of *Class A: Baseball in the Middle of Everywhere*, and his essays and stories have appeared in *Barrelhouse*, *TriQuarterly*, *Slate*, and *The Kenyon Review*. He teaches writing at the University of Massachusetts Dartmouth and lives in Providence, Rhode Island, with his wife.

lucasmann.com

Also by Lucas Mann

Class A: Baseball in the Middle of Everywhere

LORD FEAR

LORD FEAR

A Memoir

LUCAS MANN

Vintage Books
A Division of Penguin Random House LLC
New York

FIRST VINTAGE BOOKS EDITION, APRIL 2016

A portion of the text first appeared, in slightly different form,
in *TriQuarterly* #144 (Summer/Fall 2013).

The Library of Congress has cataloged the Pantheon edition as follows:
Mann, Lucas.
Lord Fear : a memoir / Lucas Mann.
pages cm
1. Heroin abuse.   2. Drug addicts—Family relationships.
3. Families.   4. Drug addiction.   I. Title.
HV5822.H4M324 2015   362.29092—dc23   [B]   2014036710

Vintage Books Trade Paperback ISBN: 978-1-101-87335-9
eBook ISBN: 978-1-101-87025-9

Author photograph © Matthew Celeste
Book design by M. Kristen Bearse

www.vintagebooks.com

Printed in the United States of America
10 9 8 7 6 5 4 3 2 1

For Josh: In loving, incomplete memory

"I know now what a ghost is. It is the person you talk to. That's a ghost. Someone who's still so alive that you talk to them and talk to them and never stop. A ghost is the ghost of a ghost. It's my turn now to invent you."

—Maria, in *The Counterlife* by Philip Roth

Author's Note

This book is about the life of a real person, my brother Josh. It draws from interviews with other real people and from his actual journals. It is not, however, an exact representation of his life. People's memories contradict one another, and many of the scenes are my imagined versions of stories they told me, complete with my own subjectivity. Almost all names, except for Josh's, as well as some small biographical details, have been changed out of respect for those who so generously shared their memories with me. I began this project in college and have been working on it, off and on, for the better part of a decade. The end product doesn't adhere to a perfectly accurate chronology. Rather, it moves between different interviews, recollections, realizations, and scenes, shaping them into a narrative of fragments that attempts to understand a life. I think that's how memory works.

LORD FEAR

Rules!!

- *ANY substance cannot be taken two days concurrently. I will keep it to twice per week, at least to start.*
- *NONE will be taken during my work (except under certain conditions).*
- *None before noon or after 9:00 p.m.*
- *None at the MET . . . don't change that experience.*
- *Remember, high or not high, there is a time and/or place for everything. It's not an all or nothing thing.*
  * REMINDER: I know I will look back on this writing with nostalgia and longing and ache. For once, I should enjoy myself while I'm still here.

I begin this story in a funeral home because I once read a Philip Roth novel that begins over a grave. Roth writes of a clenched pack of modern, white-collar American Jews shuffling their feet and talking about a man who died unfinished, and if I had to boil my brother's service down to a sentence, or an image, or just a feeling, that wouldn't be a bad way to describe it. I cannot set my story at a grave, overlooking a body, like Roth did. My brother was put into a temporary plywood box and covered in a blanket, and soon after the service he would be cremated and poured into a plastic bag. He didn't believe in God, had no interest in the traditions of a dignified burial, and, more practically, could not have been buried in a Jewish cemetery with his body intact and a large Iron Cross tattoo still visible on his right shoulder.

The tattoo was an obvious yet somehow vague act of rebellion against all the people who would soon shuffle their feet at his funeral. It came right after the eight-foot boa constrictor that he adopted and named Percy, each an ominous presence, hard to explain, better not to discuss.

Arias that I don't know and Beatles songs that I do know are playing softly because my brother liked these songs. A squat woman with bluish hair and a face like frozen dirt grabs me by the cheeks. She speaks with a thick Brooklyn accent, lots of thudding vowels and no *r*'s.

"You don't remember me, but my name's Shirley Duke and I always told your dad if you were my kid, you'd be Luke Duke," she says.

I nod and she heaves a cackle out, moves along into the crowd.

Shirley Duke will make no more appearances in this story, but she is what I remember best. I remember every word she says, and I am sure of it. The rest I try to recall, but mostly I can't. I fabricate thoughts and actions with images and insights that I wish I had. I build the moment. I assign meaning. Always, through the effort, there is Shirley's face, unimportant yet tauntingly certain.

I move past her to the very back of the room. I lean against the wall behind the folding chairs where people are sitting and talking. I have no interest in talking to anyone. I am thirteen, a good age to feel insignificant. A few feet away from me, also with her back against the wall, is Lena Milam, a newly minted thirtysomething, and between jobs. She is thin and pale. I see her and I think she is pretty in that hidden way, like in a movie before the girl gets a makeover but you can still tell. She's wearing a black silk dress that she overpaid for years ago but, until now, has never had a formal enough occasion to wear.

Lena is weeping, not loudly, thank God. Still, she feels people staring. She doesn't believe that she has earned this amount of emotion. She and my brother had been close for three years, nearly two decades ago. She is crying because someone her age is dead. She is thinking inexact thoughts about how *something* could have been done to avoid this day, a something that seems to be discussed just as flimsily by the people around her. Like we'll all soon figure out exactly what he needed and then we'll all slap hands to foreheads, saying, *How did we miss it?*

Lena is standing with Tommy Parker, my brother's best friend when he was alive. Lena and Tommy dated a long time ago. He was the first boy ever to see her naked. She remembers that she was cold that day, and tried to press her arms down on all the parts that should be covered. Neither of them looks very different now. Both are still thin and liquidy pale; both have eyes that make you worry for them. Tommy has a goatee now; he didn't then. He is enjoying the distraction of comforting this woman who he used to inexpertly kiss when she was a girl and he was a boy, an intimacy that, briefly, makes it feel as though no time has passed. Tommy hasn't yet given his condolences to my father, mostly because he's in his debt. A few months ago he asked for a loan to get him on his feet. He's an alcoholic with no job and an ex-wife who won't let him see his daughter if he can't scrounge up alimony. My father always found it easier to pity Tommy than his son. Tommy knows that and wishes he wasn't so aware of his own knowing. In a little over a year from today, he will get drunk and drive into a concrete wall off a highway in Staten Island, with a note of apology in his jacket pocket that mentions my brother's name.

Tommy walks up to me. We've met, but I don't remember it.

"Wow," he says. "You look a lot like your brother now that you're shaving."

This is embarrassing. I haven't yet started to shave, a lateness that is very troubling. Still, the comparison makes my body tense in celebration. Josh, my brother, is the most beautiful person I've ever seen, or he was. I am far too much a middle school boy to admit to myself that men can be beautiful, but, at least subconsciously, that's what I'm thinking about as Tommy speaks: my brother's beauty and what it felt like to look at him.

Behind a fake mahogany lectern at the front of the room stands a man, named Philip Goodman, who will play the emcee for the day. He begins to speak, and the rest of us fall silent. He introduces himself as a close friend of the family, meaning my father's first family, the one he had and lost before I existed. I've never seen Philip before in my life. He looks and sounds like the comedian Ray Romano, who I have an irrational distaste for, but I curb that emotion now. Philip is a good host. He's funny and conversational. He wears black jeans and a black turtleneck, which lets us all know that this is not some stuffy geriatric service, not your father's funeral, man.

Philip is thinking about how he used to babysit the dead guy. He is honing that phrase in his mind, whittling it down. It could make a really good first line of an audition monologue. *So, I used to babysit this guy who's dead.* Said offhand. Ambiguous, dark, kind of funny. He looks out at all the faces. He's a pro, an actor. More of an acting teacher now. He was on *Law and Order* once.

"Josh was a character, man," Philip hears himself saying. The audience nods at him with awed appreciation for taking on this responsibility. He likes it up at the lectern, not just because a seasoned performer knows that any accolades are good accolades, but also because he's the kind of guy who likes to help out. That's the way he always was. He used to sit with Josh on the couch until his parents got home from the movies, a small kindness but still a kindness.

My surviving brother, Dave, watches Philip, a man he loves very much. Dave lives alone and is often lonely; Philip invites him around for dinner once a week, lets him eat and talk until the loneliness doesn't feel so complete, another small kindness. Dave has sleepy eyes and full lips and a nose with a Semitic bulge that used to give him anxiety when he, too, wanted to be an actor. Now he teaches six-year-olds at a public school in Harlem and returns home to GiGi, his cat. It's a routine he likes well enough. Today is the first weekday in a long time that the routine has been broken. He will sleep in my room tonight, with me, the way he used to with Josh. I will ask him questions that he won't answer.

Dave is trying to think of something to say. He looks down at his belly, the belly of a once-skinny man whose metabolism slowed before he had time to notice. Josh got fat, too. Fatter than Dave. All Dave can focus on is how fat his brother got and how, under different circumstances, like both of them being alive, Dave would have teased him for it, and it would have been funny. He wonders how such a huge man in such a huge box will get burned down to fit into a little bag, a light load of laundry. It's like a reverse clown car, a potential joke to open with but probably not the right one. Dave decides to stay silent.

Philip continues his monologue and draws a knowing chuckle from the room. Daniel Chang is impressed by this. Daniel Chang has never performed. He's a perpetual audience member, and he sees no reason to change his role today. Daniel stands in the back, near me. He knew me when I was a baby, and once he took a picture that came out nice of me and Josh sitting on a motorcycle. His red tie is making his neck itch, and, looking at Philip's turtleneck, Daniel is a bit angry that he got dressed up for this. Few things are more annoying than dressing formal and then finding out that formality wasn't even required. He stands with Lena and Tommy. They all know one another pretty well, but Daniel is beginning to seethe at the spectacle of Lena's grief. He glances at her, then away. He keeps his arms crossed and tries to focus on Philip's stories.

Josh was a good guy. That's what Daniel would say if he got up in front of all these people. *Hey, I'm Daniel. Me and Josh were pretty close. He was a good guy.*

My mother taps me gently on the head as she walks past. She takes long strides on thin legs. I flinch and shrink from her fingers. She's bringing tissues to a woman she's never seen before, standing next to Tommy.

"Here you go," she says, holding the tissues at arm's length.

Lena looks up at her, the other light-eyed, Anglo-Saxon woman in the room, and thanks her.

My mother smiles and feels useful. She casts a glance at me, her only son, and I refuse to meet her eyes. My mother shared no blood with my brother. They had no common interests. Often he found her cold. Often, despite herself, she found him frightening. Their only connection was a man, my father, who loved them both but had loved Josh first. And me. I was a connection, a boy who could easily have been an only child and was instead obsessed with his big brother, begged for him in the moments that he was not there, said the word again and again until it was no longer a novelty—*brother, brother, brother, brother.* She remembers me running to him on wobbly legs, then feels a stab of guilt for daydreaming of my infancy on this occasion, in this place.

Once, Josh was an infant. A lovely one. Everybody who saw him swore he was so lovely that they couldn't stop looking. They kept returning to look. That's a nice memory that my father and Beth, his ex-wife, share. It is theirs. They've been divorced for a

long time and nothing much is theirs anymore, but they are sitting together now, in the very center of the first row, as though
every guest has internalized a subconscious, grief-based seating
chart and pushed the two parents into the best spots in the house.
People keep touching my father's arm and apologizing. His lips
are moving because he's imagining what he wants to say the
next time someone tells him they're sorry. *What exactly are you
sorry for?* People shouldn't say things if they don't know that
they mean them.

Next to my father, Beth shrinks down into the padding of
her seat. She's a small woman and has always found it easy to
melt into furniture and look out upon a room, undisturbed, just a
pair of eyes in the upholstery. She wants to say something but is
certain that it will sound stupid. She can picture Josh in the audience at his own funeral, laughing at his mother stumbling over
her words. The many men that Beth has taken care of in her life
are all perversely verbal, caricatures of the New York Jew who
talks and talks and eats and talks. Smart men, all of them, and
funny. Josh was the smartest one, she thinks, and the funniest.

If she had to sum up her son's existence in a sound, it would
be a burst of laughter. Even in his death, there has been laughter. Beth has already gotten a call today from Caleb, her youngest nephew, who idolized Josh and should have been catatonic.
Instead, he made her chuckle, yelling into a pay phone at a Span-
ish hostel on a post–law school trip—some story about Josh and
an elevator and duct tape. How did Caleb do that? And how, for
that matter, can Philip have such a way about him to make people grin in this room, over the body? Beth feels expectant eyes on
the back of her head. What can she say about her son? He slowed
his heartbeat down until it stopped? That isn't funny at all.

She doesn't turn her head when a woman named Sima walks
in late and sits, rigid, in the back row. Others look. Beth has
met her once; nobody else has ever seen her. She is the least

known person in this room. She's wearing black slacks and a white blouse that feels too tight now. Every time she breathes she thinks the action will break a button, send it clattering off the back of the chair in front of her and make everybody turn around, glaring, sure that the only explanation for her presence and her rudeness is that she's one of those girls he fucked and never introduced around. She is deeply aware of the fact that she is the darkest person in the room. What a light-skinned room this is. If somebody took a picture of this room, hers would be the face you found first as you scanned the image, the anomaly.

I am one of the people looking at Sima. I watch her breasts dance around in her blouse as she begins to cry. I wonder if my brother saw those breasts, naked and coffee-brown, with small, dark nipples that he put in his mouth. This has been my chief fantasy of late, nipples in mouths, a nice mixture of eating, which I know I love, and sex, which I assume I will. I see sex everywhere around me. This room is full of it, my hormones trumping my grief and then trumping the guilt I feel for not grieving hard enough.

Everyone here has had sex, some of them with each other, some of them with the dead guy. That's what I'm thinking about. I imagine my brother on top of and inside every woman that I don't know for sure is a blood relative. I imagine his body before it deteriorated, all hard lines, and I imagine hands on him. Today, when these people are done crying and shaking their heads, saying things about waste, they will go home and have sex with somebody. But not me. And sex, in my mind, equals knowledge. It's a transgression, a pleasure, two words that my life has had little of.

We're all here, I think, because of Josh's transgressions, his pleasures. I want to know them, but the time to know has passed. The plywood hides everything. A line forms at the lectern so that guests can take turns telling benign stories. The whole room nods with certainty after each one. An hour, maybe two, and then there's nobody else who has anything to say. Alone, in the back, I stare at the plywood, uneasy. I wait for something to change.

The scene is over.

It's a scene I relive often, willing it to take on new depth each time. Most of the details are made up. Most of the feelings are basic: lust, jealousy, guilt. I catalog what I can remember. I remember faces and stale air. I remember the smell of sweat and nervous bad breath. Mostly, I remember the feeling of brief, bleak community—all of us sharing in the simple awareness of the life and death of a heroin addict named Josh.

What follows is an attempt at a story about that life, that death, and the significance of both. When a man dies alone in his underwear, high, without having first found stardom to squander, of course, his significance is easy to forget.

It's the commonness that's most wrenching, Roth writes at the end of his graveyard scene.

In some ways, most ways, this story *is* pathetically common: A man dies before his time and is mourned by those who haven't died yet. It's common for a roomful of people to have each known an addict, and it's common for a roomful of people to have a reason to grieve. Nearly four hundred strangers overdosed on heroin in New York City the same year my brother did, and nearly four thousand overdosed in that decade, and it's common, I imagine, for people to Google those stats to find some solace, or at least a sense of inclusion.

It's common, too, for everyone to leave with their own memories and assumptions, to put them away in some metaphorical sneaker box in a metaphorical closet, thought about only when drunk or bored, late at night, the dead man stretching out into their kitchen, standing with them for an isolated moment before vanishing again. And I suppose it's common for the baby in the story to feel restlessness instead of sadness. To want the life remembered to be less common than every sign points to. Maybe that's the most common thing of all, embarrassingly common: my impulse to want to know more only to confirm to myself that there was someone worth knowing, worth feeling for in the way that I feel, the dull ache of my certainty that a life of importance ended unjustly.

My brother never meant to die, or at least not explicitly, so there is no note of explanation to refer to. There are only stories. The ones we tell. The ones he told. He was a writer, self-identified. He wrote songs and poems and scripts and rants and mantras. In the days after the funeral, his apartment was cleaned and all the writings he saved were collected. They were given to me, I think, because I had the fewest stories of my own to fall back on. I still wanted to know more, so maybe I would read them.

He made a lot of promises on paper, like if he wrote them down they had the greatest possible chance of coming true. His promises are, at least, a place to start.

[TYPED SHEETS, UNDATED, "SELF-INTERNAL MEMORANDUM OF JOSHUA"]:

(Carrots)

*In 2–5 years, I will have my "Valhalla" on Long Island, complete with everything—bomb home studio, a bulldog, etc. I will have created an empire (publishing, music, education, and more), press galore (celeb status), mother will be "paid back" more than she ever dreamed. I will hold tremendous power in every way and will go to Paris on a whim at least six times a year **without question**. I will have "shown them all," old employers ("The Fag Fascist"), etc. Money (tens to hundreds of millions), fame, and power. I will go even further with my **creativity in prose**. Women. Candy.*

Rules

– *There is no such thing as "no."*

– *There is no such thing as "impossible."*

– *There is no such thing as "fear."*

– *Knowledge and art are power.*

– *I am in control (destiny).*

– *Success is never a matter of "if";*

– *Only "when."*

I Will Be . . .

– *Always working (12 hours daily) / Target Oriented / IN CONTROL of all (Including the drug situation) / NO FEAR / Just People (all are).*

THIS IS MY SELF-AGREEMENT! THIS IS LIFE!

. . .

The first problem with remembering Josh is that his death immediately set to eroding the legacy of his life. *Legacy* seems like way too strong a word to use, but I cannot think of another. What I mean is that the vast majority of my memories of my relationship with him occur upon leaving the funeral home, when he was already boxed, then burned and buried. His life became increasingly overshadowed, with each passing day and then each passing year, by the only sure fact: that he died awfully.

The days after the funeral were slow. It was nearly June, and hot. I stayed home from school, sat around in my underwear, and ate leftover funeral pastries.

"You've got chocolate on your face," my father said, passing me hunkered over the kitchen table. "I'm going for a walk."

I went to watch daytime reruns, and somewhere in the middle of the eating and the watching, I began to cry for the first time since Josh's death.

My father came home and found me, tear-streaked. He'd been gone for hours and he was sweating.

"What's wrong?" he said, and then winced.

I said, "Where'd you walk?"

"Around," he said.

He went to take a shower. When he was finished, I did the same. I stood under the water for what felt like a long time. When I turned the water off, I got out and stood, disappointed, in front of the mirror, pushing at my flesh and wishing it didn't indent so easily.

Down the hallway, through the closed door, I heard my father make choking howls that he'd never made before. His sounds started low, more of a sad grumble, but then I heard his crescendo. He sounded cracked, underwater, like a broken police siren that couldn't properly warn anybody about anything. I put my head against the bathroom door and wondered when he would finish. I felt the walls vibrate, and I tried to figure out what part of his body he was slamming and what he was slamming it into. Then I heard him gasp, exhausted.

I sat on the cold tile floor and wrapped myself in a towel so that my whole body was covered, or close to it. I used to do that as a small child, pretending that I was a baby squirrel abandoned in a tree pit in a rainstorm. I used to sit, cold, squirrel-like, and wait for somebody to find me. There was no longer anyone looking. I realized that, and sat with the realization. I closed my eyes. I lay fetal and I listened to my father wind down. There was a final sound, almost a squeak, and then there was nothing. I stood and dried myself and tiptoed down the hallway to get closer to him. I leaned against the door to my parents' bedroom and I listened to him breathe.

——

My father had changed in one day. Though I wasn't sure of the specifics of the change, I was certain that one had occurred. I was impressed, maybe jealous, too, that Josh had the power to rearrange something in how our father was. Dave and I changed along with him, maybe for him, and though nobody acknowledged it outright, Josh's absence, the force of it, made a new family.

Dave became my big brother, full stop. We were, instantly, each other's only brother, each alive, and that small truth made us believe that our relationship was realer. It began when my father came through the front door on the night he found the body. He'd called ahead so we were all ready for his entrance. When he walked in, we stood like he was a TV judge. He surveyed the room and found Dave and me. He lurched at us. He caught each of us around the neck, and I think I got his left arm. He pulled our heads into his collarbones and he smelled curdled.

He spoke in a strange teapot hiss. *My boys,* he dubbed us in that foreign voice. *My boys, my boys, my boys.* And so we were.

That summer, and then every summer after, we went on vacation like a nuclear family.

Dave and I roomed together, and I remember us lying on identical, fluorescent teal bedspreads in a hotel room when I was fifteen. Our bodies pressed flat, our toes pointed, we wanted to prove who was longer.

"Stop pointing your fucking toes," he said, and reached across the space between beds to slap at my chest.

I said fuck you, but didn't hit back.

I tried to imagine us like we were both young, children of eight or nine or ten, never separated. I guessed that my father imagined the same thing every night when he popped his head into our room quick enough to see only outlines—twin beds and two boys that he made. We were all trying to stop time, or reverse it.

Really, I was a mid-growth-spurt teen, with fast-sprouting armpit hair that wouldn't stop itching and pimples like anthills on my back. Dave was balding and lumpy. He held his body with dissatisfaction, and his skin seemed to sulk, aware and ashamed of the fact that it was dripping through his thirties. The night before, I'd watched him tilt his head up and pluck nose hairs by the bathroom mirror as droplets of blood fell into the sink. Three days earlier I'd heard him shriek when he over-flossed and cut a groove in the gum skin next to one of his molars. You can't take dental hygiene lightly, he'd said. He'd become a man who lived by warnings, slathering himself in sunscreen, checking for ticks in his leg hair.

From his bed, he began to taunt me the way a brother should. He called me things that maybe he used to call Josh. Chubby boy, and then chubby boy escalated to fat boy. And then dumb, fat, little pussy. He told me I had a baby dick, and when I tried to say he'd never seen my dick, he said he saw me coming out of the shower and it made him want to laugh. I screamed that I was going to kill him.

We stood up in the middle of our room and tried to fight. He told me that if he wanted to, he could still kick my ass. He told me I was soft. I told him, bullshit, he was old.

I didn't know how to fight. I hit him with a pillow. The cotton slid across his face and made his cheeks jiggle. He swung a pillow back and I caught it, and then for seconds or minutes we were in the midst of a mighty, childish struggle. We grunted and wheezed. I felt spittle start to slide over my bottom lip, and I slurped it back into my throat too quickly, so I coughed. I managed to get an elbow into his ribs, and it felt good to know that his body was trying to recoil from mine. We spun together and we rattled the TV console, knocked a plastic-framed sailboat print off the wall.

My father threw the door open, and we looked up with sitcom guilt.

He said, "What are you, morons?"

Dave said that I started it. I disagreed, shrill.

My father began to yell, and, at first, I was frightened on instinct. But when I looked at him again he was grinning. I felt Dave's grip ease on my arm. I heard him laugh. I laughed, too. There was closeness in this tableau, no matter how bumbling it was, how ridiculous. To be wrapped in such insular, brief hate, to bruise each other until the patriarch commanded we stop—it felt like just the right kind of conflict. Boys will be boys and then they will stop and grudgingly embrace. In the morning, they will wake up and start over.

That night I couldn't sleep. My eyes were closed, but I was thinking about my imagined first sexual encounter, and about Josh—two topics that ran together easily, both so desirable and out of reach. Often, he acted out my fantasies.

Dave couldn't sleep either. I heard him kicking his sheets and I asked him what was wrong. He told me it took him twenty minutes just to get a hard-on, and sometimes it wasn't worth the effort. I lay silent, unable to empathize, still a hormonal spring trap, scared to wear sweatpants on a windy day. The pills, he said, made it like he couldn't feel.

Dave had become the most wholly dependent drug user I knew. Each morning, I watched him run his fingers through a stash of lithium, Paxil, Klonopin. The pills made his body inflate and the muscles of a young man disappear from his calves and his forearms, the way I'd seen Josh's body mutate at the end. But Dave's weren't the drugs that killed you, they were the ones that kept you alive, even though that seemed like a subtle difference.

Dave stopped talking. He blew his nose and tried to sleep. I heard him kick his covers all the way off. Then I finally dozed, thinking of Josh's arms and a woman with big eyes and no mouth. I woke to the sound of Dave screaming. I said, *What?*, and kept my eyes on the ceiling. He told me he'd had a bad dream.

"Don't you ever think about living a day and then a year and then a decade?" he asked me. "And doesn't it ever not seem worth it?"

"No," I said, not stopping to think about whether that was true.

He said he'd dreamed of a day that never ended and the sound of a motor underwater, and Josh's face hanging in the sky, laughing at him. Dave asked me if I remembered how mean Josh's laugh was. I didn't remember that. I didn't respond.

"You don't know anything yet," he said.

I think we all became quieter, though that seems impossible. It's not that we spoke less, or softly, but, still, I remember a hush.

In the years that I lived with him after Josh died, my father watched at least part of every Yankees game played. He sat on his couch, ate grapes, and watched. My mother walked past every few innings, smiled at him or asked the score when she didn't really care. Sometimes, if it was close at the end of a game, he'd tell her that and she'd sit for a few minutes before touching his shoulder and moving on.

Mostly he was alone if I wasn't with him, so I was with him a lot.

These were moments when I saw Josh, when I thought his name. His absence was heavy as my father and I watched large men dressed as boys play in the dirt. We sat close, spoke in grunts, cheered for the kind of heroes who always listened to lessons from hard fathers as they succeeded in a game marked by clean, white lines.

On weekend nights, I walked past him on my way out and

stopped to look in. I remember it—many nights distilled into just one. A room lit only by a television, his outline half in shadow, half glowing, a reflected image of Derek Jeter's face shimmering on his cheek.

I paused. My plans were to meet friends on a dark street to smoke a poorly rolled joint and talk about being stoned. And then there would be a party. And maybe there I would kiss somebody, and she would rub me over denim, though probably not. And then I would walk home late, chewing gum, looking up at streetlights like buoys in black water. My father saw me and made a sound. I saw his hands and the things that they did without him noticing. His palms turned up in a silent question as he leaned toward me.

"You going?" he asked. "It's tied still, no score."

The TV light was a wave breaking. I went to sit next to him. I put my legs up on his knees. He put his hand on my ankle. Everything was quiet and safe and still and heavy. Those were the words that I felt most, that best described growing up after Josh overdosed, after his heart slowed and then broke, after it exploded with the blood it could no longer move.

"I wasn't going to leave for a while," I said.

My father smiled and turned the volume up on the TV.

He wasn't thinking about me. I knew that. But I was there. I wondered if Josh ever sat still and silent like this. I wondered what stillness felt like for him. If it felt like effort. Years later, I would read a poem he wrote with blue pen on yellow paper, and I would picture him on our father's couch, momentarily still, his fists clenched. But I hadn't read it then, and his absence, like always, settled into the quiet.

[NOTEBOOK, MAY 1994, "MOTHER'S DAY DINNER"]:
It is strange when the pain is gone. Or maybe I'm just acclimated.
The heavy fires have dissipated and smoke remains. Smoke—still

*terrible—but not the same magnitude of the former. On this day,
a heavy ache. A sadness pulls down my psyche. A willingness to
live here, but a yearning for another reality. Or is it? A drink and
a nap hid it again. Deep down to dwell in the bowels, only to be
synthesized by the love of strength and of power.*

. . .

Time passes, nearly a decade since the death.

Our lives develop, an aging montage.

Dave marries. There is a reception at a restaurant near City
Hall. Then he gets a separation and gives up custody of the cats.
Beth decides to tattoo her eyelids to save time applying makeup
in the morning. She never regrets the decision. My father ages
gracefully. He sits in the dark less. He speed walks for exercise
and counts his calories. He meditates in his desk chair every evening with all the phones silenced, and claims to be a far less
angry person. I grow up. I am tall and thick, and I sport a patchy
beard that's mostly on my neck. I am as old as Josh was in my
early memories of him. When I'm told that I look a little like
him now, I know it's a lie but I try to believe it. I've taken some
of his old jackets—the grungy flannel, the studded punk leather.
Sometimes I wear them in front of the mirror and attempt a
sneer. My girlfriend, Sofia, watches me when I do this and she
laughs. She calls me a poseur, but she says it gently. She knows
when I'm trying too hard to be what I'm not. We are in love.

I'm a writer now, self-identified. Really, I intern and sometimes freelance for bad pay. I make a point of walking around
with a reporter's notepad in my back pocket, and I like to hit Play
at random moments on the digital recorders I fill up, just to get
the rush of hearing my voice asking a question, another's answering me. Mine is a simpleminded, mission-driven, bleeding-heart

kind of reporting. I interview people I deem sad or underserved. I valorize a local graffiti artist, triumph any and all historic preservation, generally mourn development. I stay up all night trying to talk to transgender prostitutes who work along the Hudson River, making vague promises to destigmatize them. I report on one, named Sweet Chocolate, with the cloying assertion that "standing in the solitary glow of a streetlamp, she could have passed for a schoolteacher."

A bad summer batch of heroin leads to a spike in overdoses, and I get sent to write an article about the junkies dying in Tompkins Square Park. I breathe through my mouth and remind myself that I'm heroic, and I go to the patch of asphalt where the crusties camp, asking timid questions. They invite me to sit with them. I get a little obsessed. After the article runs, I keep showing up in the park collecting quotes. There's a freelance photographer at the local weekly, a plainclothes Quaker do-gooder who has noticed my grim sincerity and has taken a liking to me. Together we go to the park, bring offerings of pizza, and gently push the victims for their stories. The leader of the group, a guy named Jewels, is as old as Josh would be, has shot up for twenty years, and carries himself, deservedly, like a veteran of a never-ending war. I like him. I ask him a lot of questions. He gives me his email address and so I send him even more questions, feel a visceral rush every time I open my in-box to his chest-puffed, all-caps answers.

I AIN'T GONNA APOLOGIZE FOR ANY MOTHER-FUCKING THING THAT I DO.

When my subjects ask me why I care, I tell them about Josh and watch their faces soften. They are kind to me for loving someone like them, is what I think, which is awfully paternalistic and probably not true, but feels great. I say his name and ask if they remember him, ask if he ever hung around the park and if they ever shared. Jewels is the only one old enough to remember that far back, but he doesn't remember much.

On a July Saturday, I leave whatever story I'm chasing and stand with my family on the patch of grass next to Josh's grave. We have the usual conversation. We talk about societal lack of compassion, the pains of the Giuliani era, and all those second-time offenders who got turned away from public methadone clinics. Et cetera, et cetera. We blame until it's time to get quiet and mourn.

We are Roth's grievers again, the way we are every year on his birthday. We are stiff with responsibility. Nobody wants to be the first to ask when we can leave or why, in the grander sense, we keep coming.

The registering once more of the fact of death that overwhelms everything, is how Roth put it. Yes, that's right.

There are six of us. Sofia is part of the group for the first time, which feels significant in a way that I'm embarrassed to think about, this reveal being the greatest intimacy I can offer. Dave's ex-wife went through the same process at the beginning. We stand in a sticky semicircle, and Beth passes around a tissue packet so that everyone is prepared for crying time. My father looks down at his son's headstone pressed flush against his mother's, does not comment on the bad arithmetic of the image.

I turn and admire the scope of this place, a cemetery so large that it has named streets within it, maps delineating neighborhoods by the front gate. I try to quantify, the way I always do, how many headstones I can count before my eyes cross on themselves, and I imagine the same image, a mouth of shark's teeth that have punctured flesh. This is just the Jewish cemetery in a town that is mostly cemeteries. The Catholic cemetery that we mock each year, with its plastic roses and giant marble crucifix headstones, is across the road, its ostentation looming on our horizon.

We stand for ten minutes, maybe. It's hot.

Then my father says, "He did not deserve this."

We all concur. No he didn't, nope, not at all, each of us tripping over one another to say it, even Sofia, who never met him, who has no idea what he did or didn't deserve, agreeing with perfect confidence. Then there's a pause.

I think this is where the story begins again for me. What I mean is that this is the moment when I decide to dig. Something infinitesimal changes in the way I grieve. Grief becomes, just for an instant, not enough. I hear myself saying that he didn't deserve to die, and I realize that this is all I know for sure about him, or all that I think I know. I have a nasty suspicion that my sadness is born from only this fact, and the vagueness of the platitude is heightened by the shark's-teeth headstones, rows and rows of deaths that should all be mourned that way, and are by somebody, by everybody. Nobody deserved it. It goes unsaid for the thousands of graves around us. But we're not grieving so much as defending him, I think, until defending him becomes the only act of remembering. We work to separate a good life, a good man, from a bad death. Once, he was young and sober and beautiful. He was pure then, and innocent, and just a regular guy, or maybe something better, and he definitely didn't deserve what came next.

"I'm losing his voice," my father says. "I can't hear him."

We all listen to the wind for a while, hissing through trees, making no noise at all as it slices between the headstones. I want thunder, but it's a clear day, a day of parched, silent sun. There is sweat running down the backs of my knees, and I reach down to scratch. Dave tries to impersonate his brother. That's not it, my father tells him, and Dave gets defensive, says it's pretty fucking close. Josh always sounded like he was going to cry on the phone; we all agree about that. You always had to ask, *Are you okay?* Then he'd get annoyed and say, *Yeah, what the hell are you talking about?* We laugh at that until the laugh dies out. "He sounded like Andre Agassi," my father says, and Beth says, "Who's that?" "A tennis player," he tells her, and she shrugs.

As we walk back to the car, Dave tells me that he has a tape of Josh's voice. It's a fake talk show that Josh used to record as a teenager, with himself as a Johnny Carson figure, Philip Goodman, the future funeral emcee, as his guest. Josh would write these long scripts, lists of questions. When Philip came over, Josh would put the tape recorder on before he even got his coat off. The tape has been sitting in Dave's desk, nestled into piles of pennies and bent index cards.

"You don't want it?" I ask.

"No," Dave says. "And don't get your hopes up. It's sort of pointless. I just figured you'd want it because you weren't there. And it seems you like to listen."

I take the tape home and put it in an old Walkman. I stare at it for a few days, and finally, alone, I sit down and hit Play. His voice sounds like I remember it, but that sound is disappointing, just a voice. I remember the sound, but I remember no thought or feeling to attach to it. I pause, wait, then start again. This time I go through the only motions I know how to go through. Somebody is real, true, verifiable, if they speak into a machine and then you write their words. I've been taught this rule. He was real. He spoke, it was audible, and I want to prove that to myself, even though I shouldn't have to.

Dutifully, mechanically, I transcribe him.

[CASSETTE TAPE, UNDATED, "THE JOSH SHOW, VOL. 1"]:

[Static. A click.]
Okay, it's back on.
[Sigh]
Great.

Welcome to The Josh Show. *Are you happy to be here?*
[Pause]
Okay, hey, Phil, I have a question. Do you like rubbing clitori?
[Giggling, from Dave in the background; no answer]
Phil, Phil, Phil, can I ask you a serious question now?
[Sigh]
I dunno, Josh, can you?
Do you like doody pie?
Come on, Josh, what kinda questions are you asking me?
[More giggling]
Okay, okay, okay, Phil, serious question. What do you think of
Toco Lewis?
What do I think of Toco Lewis? Who's Toco Lewis?
Oh, he goes to my school. So, do you ever eat titty?
[Unintelligible, frustrated exclamation]
How often do you wank? What does your dick cheese smell like?
Do you eat dick cheese? How many pubes do you have, Phil?
3,000, Josh.
3,000? You counted? How many are you gonna have by the time
you die?
3,001.
Okay, okay, okay, okay, Phil, can I ask you a serious question
now?
No, Josh, clearly you—
Do you like to eat titty?
All right, interview's over. Dave, turn the thing off.
Dave, if you touch it, I'll fucking kill you. Phil, Phil, Phil, come
on, your readers want to know. Phil, please. A serious question. Do
you like pussy juice?
[Sound of chairs moving]
Phil, Phil, wait, hey, Phil. When was the last time you rubbed
clit?
The last time you asked me, so like a year ago.

Wow, so that's a long time. What did it smell like?

Like cod, Josh.

Or haddock, what about haddock? That's a nice fish. Did the clit smell like haddock?

Josh, when was the last time you rubbed clit?

I never rubbed clit.

So instead of talking to me, why don't you go rub some?

[Pause, breathing]

Phil, Phil, Phil. Did the clit smell like haddock?

[Click]

It's tough to find nobility in the raw data, but I'm willing to try.

There is more on the tape, a few sessions' worth. I keep listening. I transcribe it all. Every page looks the same.

I try to remember something, a moment like from the tape—Josh's voice and laughter, me present this time. But memory is a hard thing to force, and, as usual, the memory I find of him centers on his absence, on the imagined. Instead of his voice, I remember *The Lord of the Rings* because the first time my father tried to explain Josh to me, he did so with a fantasy. I read the books when I was ten, eleven maybe, right when I started seeing Josh less. I was an easily frightened kid, and I couldn't sleep when I got to the Gollum passages. I imagined him hissing to me, *Precious,* a cold, gray hand snaking out from under my bed. I fled my room and found my father in the kitchen eating a banana. I told him I was scared of monsters that wanted one thing so intensely, monsters with sallow skin and no personality beyond the want, skulking around my closet. He paused, put a hand on my head, told me he had something important to say. The connection was an easy one for him to make—when a hobbit ceases to be a hobbit and becomes a creature that nobody can really know, when an addict ceases to be the person that you loved or maybe is still that person somewhere, but on the outside, the part you have to interact with, nothing remains.

It was the first time I learned to look for explanations in characters. My father sat next to me, and his arm was around me, I think. Outside, there was no moon. He spoke of how nothing is Gollum's fault, or Sméagol's for that matter—Gollum *is* fault and Sméagol is helpless. He asked if I understood, and I said I thought so.

Josh's voice on tape is not that moonless memory or that wilted character. There are funny bits to what he wrote and spoke. The part about haddock, that was good, the specificity of it. Josh was funny. I remember that, and the haddock line confirms it, at least a little. Also the part about Toco Lewis, how he just says the name like anybody should know who Toco Lewis is. I laughed at that.

On my last birthday when Josh was alive, he didn't see me and he didn't call, and my father, in lieu of giving me a talk on the birds and the bees, handed me a paperback copy of Roth's *Portnoy's Complaint*. I read the first chapter. Portnoy masturbates in a movie theater, into his sister's bra after school, into a piece of raw liver. I remember that part the most. I read it in bed and tried to imagine what it would look like. I wondered about the pleasure of it, smooth, raw meat on me, moving at my own direction. I thought for the first time of my father's lust. I asked him if Portnoy's childhood was his own. He laughed and said, "Sort of, you?"

It lent continuity, the grossness of knowing that once my father had the same shrill questions and unfulfilled desires that defined me. We were of the same type. Now, for a moment, I can see Josh as that type, as well, one with only petty shames and many questions to ask. This is an exhilarating semi-fantasy. It feels as though something, a part, has been reclaimed. He moves, briefly, away from a Tolkien brother, all morality tale and inhuman broad strokes. He fades, briefly, into a Roth brother that has to be at least a little bit closer to the truth of him.

The next night, Sofia and I have dinner with my parents, and when we leave I'm still thinking of Josh's voice.

We like walking through the city at night. We walk on quiet blocks, lined with old trees. We pass thick, square buildings and talk about the bones of them, how the beams have lasted for so long with interchangeable people moving in and out. We talk about ourselves as those people. A man moves toward us, leading a schnauzer that prances along the curb, sniffing. We crouch and it stops for us, licks my palm. We tell the man *so cute,* and he thanks us and looks really proud. He tells me that the dog likes me, that he rarely licks a stranger's hand, and now I am proud. When the man moves down the block, we talk about owning a dog, and that dog curling at our feet on the hardwood floor of our hypothetical apartment in one of these looming buildings with potted plants on the fire escapes.

This is a new way to experience New York, the place where I've always been a child. Years ago, I spent nights at Josh's apartment on the East Side, and it felt like the only time I ever really lived here, in this whole city. He lived on the second floor, and we'd crawl out his window together onto the fire escape, watch all the strangers moving beneath us. The scope overwhelmed me, so many people. It helped me to think of every one of them as him. I used to think about him walking, neighborhood to neighborhood, unafraid, the top of his head floating below all the eyes on all the fire escapes in the city.

Sofia and I stop by the river and listen to it. I tell her about that image of Josh that I used to have, the one from the fire escape. I tell her how everybody used to move like him from a distance, how every face in New York was his until right when they passed by me. She smiles at that.

The noise of a motor rumbles from the south and then a police boat passes slowly, spotlight reaching out onto black water, looking for someone. I watch the light, and I know that we'll go home tonight and lie in bed together, windows open for some breeze, music, faint and broken, coming from below. I will put my headphones on and crawl onto our fire escape. I will see the tops of heads moving, and I will think of being a child. I will listen again, grinning as my brother, a child unencumbered, bombards Philip Goodman with his questions. I will wake up wanting more.

. . .

[NOTEBOOK, AUGUST, "MY BANE BECOMES MY POWER"]:
Those who have had happy childhoods—me not being one of them—are the ones who do not ask larger questions. When you grow up a sickening wretch with CHRONIC anxiety, you develop the means to eschew foolishness.

[NOTEBOOK, UNDATED, "DREAM NARRATIVES"]:
When I was a little boy, I was afraid of the dark.

[NOTEBOOK, UNDATED, "MANIFESTO"]:
In my childhood, I studied warfare.

A long time ago, in a bright, over-cluttered apartment, Philip Goodman watches my brother prepare to torture his pet cat. Philip loves all cats, and this one, Wuzzy, is so old and pitiful that he provokes extra care. Philip is angry as he watches. He grips a pillow on the couch until it feels like he's going to rip the fabric.

"Hey, come on, quit it," he says.

But Josh's body is already coiled. Wuzzy is sleeping on the TV console, and Josh is watching him inflate and deflate. He's taken off one shoe, and now he holds it like a rock and assumes a sprinter's starting crouch, ready. He is smirking under his soft David Cassidy bob.

Wuzzy apparently does not remember, but this is what always happens when he falls asleep on the TV. Josh likes to hurl things at him. He can't throw for shit, so usually he misses and the projectile smashes into the wall behind Wuzzy, sending the cat into a panic, screeching. Which is still, Philip thinks, a kind of emotional torture.

The shoe is a brand-new Adidas, the one every kid wants. The shoe is irritating enough on its own—parents shelling out money for flashy artifice. It's easy to get frustrated. To think about how, if a kid is shown no limits, only rewards, of course he's going to use overpriced sneakers to torture creatures that are smaller than him.

Today, shockingly, Josh's aim is true. The Adidas flies as though an invisible foot far more coordinated than its owner's is controlling it. It strikes Wuzzy in the ribs, and Philip watches orange eyes open in cartoonish horror, watches the body fly into the white wall. The cat makes a feeble sound, something between a mew and a real child's cry, then falls. Josh's laughter is high-pitched. He runs toward the cat, ready to kick with his now-bare foot, really get some elevation, but Wuzzy is already hurtling himself desperately under the radiator and Josh has to settle for the pleasure of seeing him hide. He lies flat on the floor, and he pokes at his cat's face to hear the hiss. He is eleven years old, almost twelve.

Philip explodes.

"Is this the kind of person you want to be?" he says. He hears his voice rising, feels his neck hot. "You want to be a little shit?"

He is standing and pointing in Josh's face.

The boy stares back at him. He smiles. It's a hard smile, or at least it wants to be. Philip has the feeling that it's a practiced smile, something copied from hours watching TV villains with narrow mustaches and getaway choppers and cleavaged Russian mistresses. Josh shrugs. *I should smack the shit out of him,* Philip thinks. He imagines a pimpled cheek jiggling with the force of his smack.

Friends often ask Philip why he spends so many afternoons on Roosevelt Island, this quiet, homogenous cluster of middle-class high-rises. Why he is so willing to sit on a creaky floral-print couch babysitting a petulant loser while everyone else is perfectly high, lying in a circle on a carpeted floor in Brooklyn, listening to Zeppelin and drumming on their chests. The answer is complicated. Philip is loyal and he's known this family for most of his life. He grew up in Midwood, best friends with Beth's youngest brother, and remembers the feeling of being welcomed into their home, of Beth's mothering kindness toward him long before she was ever a mother. And he comes to protect Dave, too, to stop the bullying for as many afternoons as possible. Dave is a gentle child, and Philip has always felt the call to protect those who need protection.

What he tells his friends is that this is the right thing to do. Josh is fragile; his parents crave a break. It's the right thing to do to help. And there is definitely a satisfaction in feeling essential. In hearing about his essentialness, too, like he's the keystone to a building that would crash into a pile of unrelated stones without him. He can see the strain in Beth's neck when she tells him sincerely that he's the only one to get through to Josh. *He loves you, he wants to be you, he will listen, he needs you.*

And it's true. This cat-torturing boy does need.

A couple of months ago, Philip watched him stamp his rich-kid sneakers and weep, the kind of ugly weeping where your eyes almost close and your mouth twists in on itself like you're about to puke. Philip stood in the doorway of the apartment. It was wintertime. It was snowing. My father and Beth, after all the awkward silences and the nasty whispers, were going to take a vacation. They were going to salvage things and leave the boys with Philip so that he could provide his own kind of salvaging.

The phone rang from the airport—all the flights were canceled because of the snow; the parents would be stuck at home. My father went to put his coat away. Beth sat on the couch, turned on the television, and tried hard not to look anyone in the eyes. Philip was silent but relieved, already thinking of a weekend free of forced father-figure bullshit. Dave gave a disappointed shrug and sat down next to his mother, asked for the remote.

Plans had been changed; everybody would go on living.

But when Philip looked at Josh, there was darkness. He really thought that word, *darkness,* a metaphorical shadow on the kid's face, so apparent that it became visibly real. It felt too big and melodramatic a word to describe a cranky preteen, but what else? He was like an old clock spring, winding tighter, tighter.

Josh began to howl, a strange mimic of the wind outside as the storm picked up. When he ran out of breath, it seemed like it might be over, but then he gasped and howled again.

Stop, Philip thought. *For everyone's sake, don't be embarrassing. Realize how embarrassing you're being and then stop it.*

Josh did not stop. He kicked at the coffee table as he ran to his bedroom. The family trailed him. Philip watched. He watched Josh writhe on his bed, screaming the word *no* until it sounded like he had a stutter. It was the kind of gutted repetition that actors utilize in movies when something *awful,* like genocide awful, has happened, and even then you wonder if they're overdoing it. Philip always preferred subtlety on-screen, in general.

There should be some correlation between the seismic effect of an event and a person's reaction to it. Looking at Josh, Philip didn't see a logical correlation to anything.

Beth tried to move in on her son, to love him, wrap him up. It was a sweet impulse, but Josh was too big for the moment to look sweet. He was a broad-shouldered boy, a bit chubby, larger already than his mother as she tried to hold him in small, shaking hands. She wanted to swaddle him, her baby, but he wasn't a baby and she couldn't. Philip watched her roll off, then sit next to him on the bed, reaching out every few seconds to touch him on his heaving back and see if he felt it. Josh hid his face in a pillow, but he kept screaming. It looked like the sound was escaping through his ears.

Dave lingered by Philip's leg like the cat. He reached up, pawed him, and wanted to know why all of this was happening. *What's wrong with him?* is what he said. Philip didn't answer. He patted Dave's head. He wondered what strange feat of genetics could make one boy so solid, so right, and send another shrieking and babyish into puberty. It felt important to let Dave know, in some way, that he wasn't implicated in this. That Josh was the kind of flawed that provides no lineage or explanation.

My father stood over the bed for a while, palms up like he was asking a question. His shoulders, broad like his son's, were tense, almost at his earlobes. He coughed and shook his head, and then walked past Philip out of the room. Philip watched his measured steps down the hallway to the closet, where he retrieved his winter coat. He put the hood up over his ears and walked out into the snowstorm. Josh didn't notice, didn't hear anything but his own volume. How long was he going to scream?

Josh wanted to be with Philip. That's where the tantrum came from, and Philip was keenly aware of it in the moment. Josh wanted his parents gone. He wanted to sit next to Philip and feel his essence, his coolness, as though some osmosis could happen there in the apartment and Josh could become him, an instant solution to the problems of growing up. That's what all twelve-year-old boys desire, right? To not be themselves and not be their parents; to instead be something mercifully in between? Philip could relate to the impulse. It was the way that Josh went about his desire that lurched past pitiable into repulsive. Desire is only desirable when muted, the way Philip had learned to look at women, restraining himself enough for them to notice the restraint and grow curious.

Josh's hand began to bleed.

Maybe his knuckles had scraped his bed frame or the plaster of the wall. There were tear streaks on his Kiss sheets, snot stains across Gene Simmons's scowling face. And now smeared drops of blood. Philip thought of Beth. He pictured her later that night, after he'd been blissfully relieved of his charge, cleaning her boy's fluid like he was an infant, while my father high-stepped through the snowdrifts until the embarrassment was over. It was a triptych that Philip wouldn't forget, that he would relay in detail to anybody who ever asked about Josh, the defining images: A boy writhing. His mother cleaning. His father ashamed.

Philip continues to try. For years. He continues to tell himself that it is the right thing to do to try.

He watches movies with Josh when Dave is out with friends and the apartment feels too big.

He reads the overwrought poems Josh writes and he doesn't make fun of them. "There's talent here," he says. "And sensitivity. Girls love sensitivity."

He teaches Josh the drums, even though he's never taught and never plans to teach again. Philip's good, but there are plenty of real teachers out there. He even offers up the man who taught him years ago, but my father begs, tells him that a real teacher will lose patience, tells him that it has to be Philip or nobody. So Philip tries. He sits on Josh's bed and listens to him beat on the brand-new kit that my father bought him before he'd ever played. He tells him, "Good," when he finally masters the easiest of Beatles songs. He smiles when Josh says, "I'm going to be a fucking rock star." When Josh earns his way into the High School of Music and Art, Philip never mentions that hardly anyone tries out for drums.

They settle into a rhythm, the two of them. Josh writes, Josh plays, Philip listens. He claps obligingly. He agrees with Beth that maturity is happening when it isn't. He is patient. But the longer their relationship lasts, the more afternoons pile up, identical, the heavier his effort feels.

The interviews are the last monument to his patience. *The Josh Show*—who else would be the guest?

Philip sits in the kitchen. He shuffles his socked feet on white tile. He rests his elbows on the table and lets the weight of his body fall. He tries to let the questions wash over him, like a meditative kind of thing, an almost gentle buzzing. Give one-word answers every few seconds, fall into yet another rhythm, and then it will be over.

Josh looks the way he always looks when everyone in the room has tired of him. He's leaning forward at Philip, palms flat on the table. His eyes are wide, his face skin stretched tight, manic. Philip thinks of it like a dead sprint distilled into a facial expression.

Phil, Phil, Phil, Phil, Phil.

Josh is bleating at him. He says something about tits, then something about pussies. Now he's asking Philip what pussy smells like. Again. Philip hears himself saying, "Like cod," which is funny, he thinks. He smiles to himself. He has always been told that he's funny. He understands the mechanics of humor. It has to be quick and effortless, a shift snuck into an unsuspecting conversation, not a barrage of dirty words thrown until one sticks. Josh is saying *clit*, over and over. Other words, too, but he's saying *clit* the loudest, with real glee. Philip wants to get close to the tape recorder and say with slow, unmistakable enunciation, *Josh, it doesn't get funnier the more you do it.*

The last time Philip came over, he brought his girlfriend. Josh said the same words to her. He talked about fingering pussies and laughed as he mimed the gesture. She gripped the handle of her coffee mug tight, and Philip had to watch little veins pulse on her hands.

"I think we've got somewhere to be," she said. "Philip, don't we?"

"Where you going?" Josh said. "Where you going, guys? Where you going?"

Philip leaned in close and hissed, "Stop it, Josh. Come on, man, stop it."

"You going home to finger her pussy?" Josh said.

Even when they made it to the elevator, Josh was still audible. He was leaning out the door into the hallway—"Phil, hey Phil, where you going?"

When the elevator door closed, Philip hugged his girlfriend and she exhaled.

"He's just too old to be that way," she said. "It's not right."

Phil, Phil, Phil, okay, hey Phil.

Josh is still going in the present. His giggle has become a shriek. He stamps his feet on the tile floor in a happy way. On the wall behind him, thin-stemmed wineglasses shake with the force of his stamping, make little plinking noises. His body is powerful. He has begun to pack his broad frame with new, adult muscle. Pectorals push against his T-shirt. He's no longer a chubby boy. If Philip had just met him today for the first time, there maybe would have been that stab of jealousy that occurs whenever a man in his thirties passes a sculpted teen on the street, the knowledge that he could never return to that ideal now even if he tried. But this is Josh. Philip knows Josh. He imagines leaning across the table, putting his fingers on Josh's biceps, and finding it to be slick, inflated plastic like a pool toy. He imagines pricking the biceps with his fingernail and watching the body deflate.

Phil, are you listening? Phil, Phil, Phil.

His patience is gone.

Phil, when was the last time you rubbed clit?

Philip hears his own voice cut in despite himself, chiding, *When was the last time* you *did?*

At first it feels good to point out that Josh has never rubbed a clit in his life, to give him pause, if only for a second, but then it feels sad.

Philip stands. He hears his own voice again, and it sounds like an older man's.

"We're done here," he says. "Turn the thing off."

He's out of energy. He leaves fast. Josh watches him from the doorway, smiling, certain that he will see him soon.

Josh never tracks him into the hall, never rides the elevator down with him. Never wants to hang out at Philip's apartment. Never wants to be taken out for dinner, or to a ball game, even just for a walk along the river. He's supposed to be a musician, but he never goes to a club to see a show. There's a whole city around you, Philip told him once. All these lives, all these fucking interesting people with things to tell you. Josh shrugged, said fuck all those people, grinned a stupid grin. Philip grins in the elevator, thinking of Josh as some iron-pumping, emotionally unstable Rapunzel, waiting helpless, high above any intrigue or danger, for a visitor who is willing to climb.

Philip will climb again, he knows that. He will be asked and he will oblige. And it will be the same, static and tense. Minutes will pass slowly, and Josh will be what he always was. Because the thing about living is that it's hard. Philip is thirty-three and still trying to make art, pay his rent, be good to a woman for an extended period of time. He still gigs on the drums, sits sore at the bar after his sets, paid in watered-down drinks. He writes songs and scripts, and he hopes that they'll someday be famous. He auditions for all the small hoodlum parts available to angular, olive-skinned men. Josh has a life planned that looks something like Philip's. Being creative and being handsome and being a man, a fully developed human being beyond his mother's apartment. Philip shakes that notion away. Josh, adult, paying bills, making art, not merely imitating the shell of an artist's presentation—every detail of the idea is insulting to Philip, insulting to his ambition, to the work it takes to be him. It's a hypothetical that feels like it will always remain one.

The elevator opens at the lobby, and then Philip is outside in real, dirty New York air. He walks along the river, watches the chop. He thinks about the tapes, about how this will be the last time with the fucking tapes, even if Josh begs him. There will be no more recorded evidence of their time together. Good. The tapes will disappear, like songs do, like poems, and eventually he'll stop feeling the need to try.

Philip's cat hisses at me. It shakes its ash-gray bulk and sends tufts of matted fur up into the air. I sneeze and glare at it.

"You heard the tapes, right?" Philip is saying. He is sunken into his couch along the back wall of a tiny living room in a rent-controlled apartment near Prospect Park. "You get what I'm talking about, right?"

I feel myself nodding. Then I sneeze again.

"Sorry," I say. "Allergic."

Philip nods at this, so I keep the motion going, and we bob our heads at each other for a while. He wears torn black sweatpants and a white T-shirt with faded words written along the chest. He'd just come back from a run when I met him on the stoop. He lives by the maxim that the older you get, the healthier you have to be. I don't know how true that maxim is, but he assures me that someday I will.

A decade ago, I watched him conduct my brother's funeral with his black turtleneck and gentle eyes, and I assumed so much. And in the way that memory can make us so certain about assumptions, I became certain that if we were to meet again, he would be, if not physically the same, on the same emotional pitch, waiting to continue in the sincere, near-reverent manner that I left him in. He was the orchestrator of everyone's last kind speech about my brother, and whenever I try to find that memory, all those stories with their sweet, melancholy jokes, their assertions of transcendent qualities possessed only by Josh and the absolute shock at the loss of him, Philip's face is one of just a few sure things. He has refused, all afternoon, all through our hours of talk stretching out in this cat-dandered apartment, to live up to any aspect of how I remember him or, more precisely, how I remember the way he remembers. And why should he? It's not his responsibility to reshape what he felt, yet I still feel let down.

There had been a conversation in my head before this meeting, and it was nearly symphonic in its good vibes. I pictured the way my laugh and Philip's would sound together. They would sync up, is what I thought. They would come easily because Josh made us both laugh. And there would be a familiar quality, because I've been told that my laugh echoes my brother's, and he would surely recognize that. I have actually been waiting for Philip to say something funny, so that I could laugh sincerely at what he said and then he could say, *My God, I just heard him, just now, in you.*

He's glancing at my notes, willing them to end.

"I'm not sure what you want," he says. I hear his feet shuffle on the throw rug beneath him. "You want some more water?"

He's up, bounding the corridor to his kitchen. Old wood groans under him. His legs, still boyish, elastic and thin, step around and over a life's worth of sentimental debris. There are records with loved, worn covers. There are books, too, stacks of them that would ordinarily render me grudgingly impressed, and I can see once-bright Post-its sticking out above the pages that he wants to remember most. I find only smugness in the warmth of this place, the years that he has lived within these walls and will continue to do so, the art he has accumulated, the smiling expanse of pictures on every countertop, the satisfied routine of his existence.

I hear Philip drop a mug and stumble around in his kitchen. I hear him say, "Shit, shit." When he comes back, he eases down onto the couch with a sigh. I try to look at him hard. I have more questions lined up. Possibilities include: Do you think he thought that all great artists get high? And, Are there times when you think of him the most? Why? And, Do you remember what you said at the funeral? Do you remember what I said?

I ask none of these and instead ask a question that I know will be my last. If we were boxing, and it feels a little as though we are, this would be a haymaker thrown rounds too early by a fighter who is tired and just wants to hear the sound of something heavy connect.

"Do you think you loved him?" I ask, looking past Philip at the cat who has fallen asleep, face pressed into its own stomach.

I ask him only because the answer will be yes, and, sure, it's an aggressive, manipulative use of the word *love*, but really, what isn't? I want, at least, some agreement, so I can end this fumbling interview on my terms, terms that happen to be widely accepted terms for all people, and thus are irrefutable. Love is so much better than any alternative, and so we say it.

Philip digs his hands into the fur on his cat's head until everything but his wrist has disappeared, and still it doesn't wake.

"For me, he was impossible to love," he says. He stares at me and then blinks. "You have to know somebody if you're going to love them, or else to say you do is bullshit. I don't want to bullshit you."

He keeps staring, looking for agreement. I nod for him, regret it.

"Some people aren't meant for that," he says. "You and I have been sitting here for a few hours, and I just connected with you more than I ever did with him."

My favorite part of Nabokov's autobiography, *Speak, Memory*, is the way he nestles the idea of memory into so many different images. There isn't one central metaphor; memory is not merely an ocean or an ever-splendored thing. Instead the whole book reaches for metaphor again and again, always with a new image to put to a word that is invisible and ineffable on its own. He writes of the hand of memory, the horizon of memory, the way memory can crumble. Memory as a backdrop, an eye, a glass cell, an entire city, an engraved stone, a stack of books. He settles on none of these, never seems to reuse or even refer back to an old metaphor when trying out a new one.

Memory is a fight. That is what I believe in this moment.

Memory is the back-and-forth pull between Philip and me, the struggle that hangs over his coffee table, each of us with a quiet need to be right. The problem is that no memory is entirely right, just as the meaning of the word can always change. And what I'm trying to do, let my memory of one life meet and mingle with others, is a flawed endeavor, pretending that a peace exists within acts that are not peaceful.

Josh was a boy who inspired, who deserved, love. No, he never was.

I get up to leave fast, and soon Philip and I are at the door to his building, shaking hands. He grips tight and tells me that I'm starting to look like my father. I mumble something about how, yeah, people have said that, and then something else, funny I think, about how there are worse things to hear but not many.

He stands in the doorway and watches me leave. I turn back and wave, he reciprocates, and then I'm gone. It's only once I get around the corner on my way to the F-train that I realize we never spoke of needles or death. The only part of the story that I'd been sure we would cover, we didn't. That should be a good thing. The character he gave me, the version of my brother that he made and I took and then wanted to give back, was not a dying junkie. But the death *was* there. It didn't have to be spoken. It loomed, the result that all of Philip's anecdotes about the things broken in Josh served to explain, so that he could never be just a young boy frightened or a teen overcompensating. Maybe it really was that way when Philip lived it, this awareness of the cracks, or maybe it came later, after Josh died the way he died, and all the details in Philip's mind lined up to prove that he had known something all along, that he hadn't been fooled at all.

Memory desires, above all, to be right.

[POEM, UNDATED, "THE DREAM OF 4/17"]:
Train tracks. Trying to jump the train, can't.
Trying to shower (naked), public place (Lincoln Center).
Warnings about those after us in the train yard (Father figure?)
Signs of yesterday refuse to give up. I must think of it like this.

It seems so real but that is only the physical appearance, an incorrect one at that. Psychological mistakes. Under it (or above it) is reality. Not bad. Not good. But not what dreams speak of. Rational.

I am in a Chinese restaurant on Sixth Avenue. I am four years old, or maybe I'm five. I am young enough to kick my feet in my chair and feel them swinging high above the floor. Josh and I are alone because he's my babysitter, and that makes this night take on a hazy, buzzing quality, every atom in the air, on my skin, electric. He's wearing sunglasses, yellow-tinted aviators, even though it's nighttime and we're indoors. We're eating crunchy noodles as loud as we can, and he sees me staring at the glasses so he lets me wear them. I put them on, and I can't see anything, hardly, just the outline of his cheeks and his teeth smiling into the dark yellow. He takes them back, and I ask him, *How can you see; how is that possible?* He shrugs and I watch his shoulders move, and I think of watching boats on the river when it's choppy, the way they heave up and settle themselves down so perfectly with each wave. I think everybody else in the restaurant is looking at us, looking at him, and seeing the same thing.

"You want to hear a joke?" he asks me, hunching forward.

The way I remember it, this is the first joke I have ever been told. I nod my head that I want to hear it. He whispers and we lean closer to each other.

"So there was a faggot who was on a football team," he begins. "But he didn't realize that he was a faggot yet."

I don't know what *faggot* means, but I like football and I can tell by his face, his grin every time he says the word, that it's a word of consequence, dangerous in a way that I cannot articulate my desire for. He says it quieter than the other words, but louder somehow.

"He always played tight end when he was in the closet," Josh continues. "But what do you think happened when he came out of the closet?"

The question doesn't resonate with me at all. I don't know what closets have to do with football, or why he would have been in one and not on a field. And when Josh answers the question, "He switched from tight end to wide receiver," I am no closer to understanding but I have no wish to understand because now he's laughing and his laugh sounds like applause, or it doesn't sound like it but it feels like it. I laugh with him and my laugh is higher, but I like the way our laughs sound together, careening off the walls and the tables, building force as he asks, gasping, if I get it, and I tell him yes.

I ask him to carry me home on his shoulders because I'm exhausted and I know that he can do it. I bob through New York, and I think of pictures of men riding on elephants that Josh brought back from his trip to India. I whisper something about elephants into his ear, and he holds his arm out in front of us like a trunk and makes a trumpeting sound. He begins to buck and heave a little under me, so I hold tight around his neck. I don't know what I'm feeling, but I feel it deeply, the view from his shoulders, his voice floating up to me, the streetlights above us, stretching out like fingers into the black.

My favorite of Nabokov's metaphors is this one: *Nothing is sweeter or stranger than to ponder those first thrills. They belong to the harmonious world of a perfect childhood and, as such, possess a naturally plastic form in one's memory, which can be set down with hardly any effort.*

It's like hands in newly laid concrete, how fast you can leave a print and how long that print will last, prints that I experienced without any thought that the memories might run out or shift in meaning once I understood all the words. I like to think that these are pure, purer somehow than Philip's memories, because

Nabokov says that only as we age do our memories get *choosy and crabbed*. But I already asked Philip what he thought he knew, and now, even as I don't want them to be, his memories are mine, at least a little bit they are.

I get out of the subway on Sixth Avenue, where once I rode on my brother like he was an elephant. The Chinese restaurant is gone and has been gone for many years. It was a Foot Locker, then an Arby's, and now it's an enormous nail salon. Through the windows I see dozens of women, spread out and stooped over other women's feet, mouths sheathed in blue paper masks, eyes down. All of this feels so trite to observe. Time has passed. New things have sprouted where old things died, and so it's harder to see the old things. I remember myself leaning down over my brother, my elephant, on this block so that I could hear him. I remember him saying, "Do you love me?" Maybe there was need in his voice, a need for easy validation, but I don't remember it that way. I just remember saying yes and then rising back up as tall as I could, putting my fat little arms in the air, and trusting that he wouldn't let me fall.

. . .

My father keeps beer in the fridge for me. He doesn't drink, really, and I don't live with him anymore, but I think he likes that I come over and, when I do, he can say, "There's beer."

I live in Brooklyn with Sofia now. There is no reason for me to have post-work beers with my father, but I do, three, four days a week, settling into that familiar hollow space on the couch next to him. I text Sofia that I'm working late, cold-calling for the nonprofit that I cold-call for, or chasing an interview for a story. Usually, I stay until right before the B-train stops running. I hurry to catch it and feel guilt, though I'm not sure what for.

Dave has been living here, mid-divorce, and the three of us sit in a triangle. He wears a moth-holed red sweater that used to be my father's. He's reading an old paperback copy of *Herzog*.

"Read something else," my father says.

"Why?" Dave says. "I like classics."

"It's a cliché."

"Just because I'm divorced?" Dave says. "Or narcissistic? Or Jewish? Is this a self-hating thing?"

I laugh.

"Have you even read it?" Dave snaps.

"Of course," I lie. "It's about an unhappy, divorced Jewish guy. It's a classic."

"You want to watch a movie?" my father says.

This is a common progression. We are readers and watchers. We compete with knowledge of the art we consume. We quote lines and challenge one another to identify the source. We play that game where one person names a movie, then the next an actor from that movie, then the next another movie that actor has been in. We play in endless circles. We speak of the world in archetypes. In the movie of our family, we have decided, Albert Finney will play my father because of the eyebrows. And Paul Giamatti will play Dave—he doesn't like that. And Seth Rogen will play me.

My father bought himself a John Ford/John Wayne DVD box set, and we've been sporadically making our way through each of the Westerns. He loves John Wayne movies, that whole parched-earth, stoic morality thing. I like them, too. Dave, not as much. He finds them all surface, resents that we're supposed to assume that there's depth under monosyllabic restraint.

Last week we watched *Stagecoach*, laughed when Wayne faced Claire Trevor, told her, "I know all I want to know."

Josh used to write movie scripts. I don't know if he ever finished one, but he left behind ideas, story lines, short scenes, title pages with huge, bolded type. When I slept over at his apartment, I would fall asleep on the couch to the sound of his typing. In the morning, he printed what he wrote on long, perforated sheets. He let me rip the pages apart, and then sometimes he let me read aloud the side characters, usually women, while he voiced the protagonist. He wrote about the city at night. He had consistent themes and types. There was a drug lord named Alonso, a tortured DEA agent named Lance. Men with clenched jaws and burdens unspoken. I pictured them all with his face.

I have his old scripts now, at least the ones he saved. They're mostly just first scenes. They open in the early morning hours, predawn, and make some reference to most of the city that never sleeps being asleep. He favored searching cameras, lots of sweeping across the Manhattan skyline, spotting one light on in a building, zooming in fast to find a young man, handsome, well-dressed, once described as "conservative" in look and behavior, about to get caught up.

Ah, says the voice-over in the last script he ever began. *This is just who I was looking for.*

It's an appealing place to start, a nice trope to think about: the heartthrob facing dangers long after everyone else has gone to bed. Never mind the cheesy titles—*The Loophole. Executive Justice. Heaven, Hell and the Witness Protection Program.* Focus on the ideal.

Tonight, I'm expecting a later John Wayne effort, *The Searchers* maybe, but my father says he has a surprise and pulls out an unmarked DVD of never-watched home movies that he got converted. They are predictably benign. There's a scene of my second birthday, and we laugh at the way I shovel cake into my mouth. There are shots of my father trying to film a boat in the distance, his voice from behind the camera saying, "I can't figure the thing out."

Then static, then a new scene.

The new scene is grainier; I'm not sure why. It's set in a rented summerhouse on Long Island, walls the color of moldy bread and an oblong living room with a piano in the corner. The camera is positioned on a counter, pulled back from the action. From the moment the camera turns on, there is music. Josh sits at the piano and plays, arms dangling out of a red tank top.

"He taught himself how to play the piano," my father says, sitting next to me. "Nobody taught him that. He taught himself."

It's just after sunset in the video. The shot looks candlelit but there are no candles. Josh begins to play "Let It Be," even slower than the original, not plodding, though, sensuous. I hear voices from behind the camera begin to sing. A back swoops in, arms holding me, and then I'm placed on his lap as he plays. He looks over me at the camera. I look where he looks, and for a second both of our eyes are facing out, glowing. Josh begins to sing softly. I can't hear him over the voices closer to the camera, but in the video I hear him and my body sways with what the sound must be. I collapse into him, and I put my head on his chest like I can feel the music vibrate out of his skin.

The clip is only a few minutes long. There's no progression, just a steady camera fixed on one point where Josh happens to be sitting, like a Warhol movie, but nostalgic. Then, static.

My father has begun to cry. He cries only at films, sometimes books.

"Movie star, right?" he says.

"Totally," I say.

It feels important for him to say and for me to agree with. We are, after all, cultural consumers in this family. We put stock in our taste. We find beauty there, in the proof of knowing what we saw and whether it was good.

There's a particular moment halfway through Roland Barthes's *Mourning Diary* that I often return to. Ten months after his mother's death, he watches an old movie. It's a Hitchcock mystery from the forties. As he watches, he feels no escapist joy; but what he records instead is the soothing sensation of finding his dead mother in Ingrid Bergman, who doesn't look anything like her. On-screen, captured, he sees: *her lovely, simple hands, an impression of freshness, a non-narcissistic femininity*—his mother in words that he hadn't yet thought to use, in a place he hadn't been trying to look for her. That rings true for me. Not the exact connection that he made but the fact that he made it, those general qualities that an icon can be a vessel for, so much brighter and easier to see in moving strips of light.

I have found my brother in Patrick Swayze, Brando, John Travolta (in that movie where he drives a taxi and raises Kirstie Alley's child), Steve Guttenberg, Bruce Lee, Heath Ledger (before the obvious association), Elliott Gould, Tupac, Spencer Tracy, Kenneth Branagh in *Hamlet,* Laurence Olivier in *Hamlet,* Warren Beatty, Jean-Paul Belmondo, and Leonardo from the live-action *Teenage Mutant Ninja Turtles* movie. He's in their lips or their shoulders or their eyes; their confidence, their contradictions, their promise.

Now, in this little room, in the dark that is so familiar, as my father weeps like that time he took me to see *Streetcar* as a kid, I'm seeing my brother as himself, or it seems like it, at least. I think he would have liked that, the meeting of fantasy and reality, captured, vivid, in moving strips of light. It's flickering, fast, but I see him.

This is a scene as I envision it:

Josh is leaning against a puke-colored locker, something out of a John Hughes fantasy, his wispy beginnings of armpit hair catching the fluorescent hallway lights, poking out from a cutoff Zeppelin T-shirt. Drumsticks, his very first pair, used gifts from Philip Goodman, writhe in his hands. He keeps a beat on his thighs, wooden tips clicking on tight black denim. He doesn't smile and he doesn't speak to anybody, because he's concentrating. When the bell rings for first period, he sighs and tosses his head back, his mane of hair bouncing above his shoulders. He puts the sticks in his back pocket. He walks past Daniel Chang toward homeroom. Daniel has been staring at him. When Josh gets close enough to make eye contact, Daniel panics, presses himself up to a water fountain and watches with a tilted head, slurping until Josh disappears.

This scene blends into one of a school bus, packed. Josh is there again, drumsticks blurring, bare arms dangling, body erect. Most of his middle school peers are watching him as they bump around the three-mile loop of Roosevelt Island, where they all live stacked in new high-rises. Josh returns nobody's gaze.

Daniel Chang is in the back, watching Josh over the top of his seat. Daniel is newly immigrated, still friendless. Watching Josh provides him with a rare feeling of inclusion. Everyone else seems to be watching—the boys that try to hide it, the popular girls that seem to move and lust in a pack. Daniel sees what they see, and thinks that if Josh turned and looked back at him, his whole life might be different. The bus stops in front of Josh's building, and he's up, two bouncing strides toward the door, and then he's gone until tomorrow. Exhale.

By November, it's already freezing cold at dusk. Daniel is standing on the bike path along the East River, and he's shivering because this is the cusp of his first New York winter and he doesn't yet own a jacket. In thin jeans and a sweatshirt, he tries to stop shaking and thinks he can feel his newly descended testicles rising back into him like the lotto numbers that his mother watches sucked into tubes every evening. He's here because his first friend has brought him with the promise that others will be here. One of those others is Josh, leaning over the metal railing, spitting into the water. As a pinkish, polluted sunset shimmers across midtown Manhattan, Daniel Chang is introduced to Josh. They face each other, and Daniel wills himself to say, "Hi, I'm Dan," because he has decided Dan sounds better than Daniel.

Josh looks him up and down, more down since Dan is nearly a head shorter than him. Time is, of course, slow. Maybe they can hear water like a tongue slapping the pylons below them.

"Danny Boy," Josh says finally. Then he smiles, so Dan smiles, too, until his teeth get cold and he knows he's held it too long. He jerks his head down to look at his Keds like he's never noticed them before.

A relationship develops like whirring 16mm footage, uncut but sped up. They aren't best friends, but they're around each other more and more—a bigger boy and a smaller boy walking along the East River as the sun sets and rises and sets again. In Dan's apartment, the air is quiet and stale, both his parents either working or worrying. He hurries back out into the city, where Josh is, and motion returns as they explore a New York that has the gritty swagger and grayed color palette of a Cassavetes film. Dan watches Josh as they mature together, remembers the details.

They are seventeen now, maybe eighteen, and he has followed Josh to a party full of kids with famous parents and paint on their pants. Dan goes to the local public high school, but Josh goes to the magnet art school to play the drums every day. Dan has no affinity for art of any kind, but he likes the word and the word works for Josh, with his pouting lips, his all-black wardrobe, his seeming detachment from responsibility.

The party is in a Manhattan apartment overlooking Central Park, and Dan scans the walls speculating on the value of everything. It's one of those apartments that was built at the turn of the century, with a maze of extra rooms once meant for cooks and maids and sets of grandparents. Now it's a place to get high and then get lost looking for the bathroom. Dan walks past a room full of nude African statues, watches two pasty strangers making out, unable to look away until one of them sees him and stares back. Dan shoves his palms into his blue jean pockets and wanders on. He feels two crumpled bills and what he briefly hopes is a quarter but soon realizes is a nickel. Everyone around him is talking about beauty—the beautiful feeling of a drug he's never tried, the beautiful sound of the keyboard on a record he hasn't heard of, the beautiful way light functions in some movie with a French name. He thinks of the conversations that Josh must have during the long school days when Dan isn't present, every word a reference to something else, a language that one needs to be initiated into.

Dan enters the living room. He hears his sneakers squelch in spilled wine, panics, and then finds Josh. Josh is standing in the center of the room, and if he isn't bigger than everyone else, he at least seems to be. He has begun to devour weight-lifting handbooks and drink protein shakes. He writes workout plans, laminates them, shows them to all his still-scrawny friends. They, too, seem to be written in an alien tongue. A shield of muscles tugs at a shirt that Dan remembers being loose once.

The lifting was a brilliant decision. Dan can see that. What's more avant-garde, in a room full of the concave, self-titled avant-garde, than looking like the hypothetical bullies they're rebelling against? Sure enough, Dan sees clusters of these too-hip skeletons edging toward Josh, curious, wanting to be near him, to brush a shoulder of that bulging shape just to see what it feels like.

Josh is holding a beer that he hasn't sipped from in hours. Beer is all carbs and the loss of control. The loss of purity, really, both mental and physical. Josh is pure. Dan watches Josh's free hand, where there is all the evidence of sober concentration. He keeps up a steady, complicated rhythm on the arm of the velvet couch in front of him, something that could appear to be a fidget if you weren't looking closely enough.

A girl interrupts Dan's sight line. She walks up to Josh and offers him a cigarette. He scoffs and says something shitty about how he prefers air. Dan thinks that this might be the most beautiful girl he's ever seen, and though that's something he thinks often, he is ready to stand by his assessment in this case. Her hair is somewhere between red and brown and her lips are red. Her jeans are tight, tight from the ankle to the crease of her knee to the controlled swell of her ass. David Bowie is on her T-shirt, bright blond hair, bright blue makeup. Josh wears makeup. He doesn't talk about it but Dan sees it. Does she know that? Does she like it? Is it a Bowie thing?

Dan tries to catch his friend's eye to give a look that says, *Holy shit, that's the most beautiful girl I've ever seen.* He begins a little wave, but feels his hand suspended up by his shoulder and aborts. Hands back in pockets, he watches the girl ask Josh questions. *Are you having fun?* Leaning closer. *Do you ever smile?* Fingertips on his unresponsive arm. *Take me somewhere quiet?*

Dan is still, like if he moves it might ruin something. Josh whispers an excuse in her ear, and she has the look of someone rejected for the very first time. She pulls her fingers back from his elbow. Josh smiles over her head at Dan and makes a face like he's nauseated by her presence. Dan is furious at the injustice of the world and the different ways that different people are allowed to experience it. Josh struts over to him.

"Nothing worse than a drunk chick," he says. "That's a woman without dignity."

"Yeah," Dan says.

Josh surveys the room, says something about weakness. We are too good for this place, he tells Dan, and Dan is no longer angry. Together they strut to the elevator, then out onto the street. They walk through Central Park. It's black and there's scuffling in the shadows. Dan thinks he can see people, thinks he hears running footsteps, but he's not sure. The park at night is a prime example of the kind of place Dan's parents have told him not to be, all shadow. Josh walks fast, steps loudly, doesn't care who hears him. Dan hurries to keep up.

Four years later, they are still friends, more so than ever, if only because of proximity. Other friends have moved far away to college, and so Josh and Dan are left together, always a pair now.

They're in Chinatown at a dim sum joint with tiny wooden tables and tiny plastic chairs, where Josh is the only white guy. He seems to enjoy that; it's a scenario he cultivates often. He sits splayed and satisfied, the whole restaurant reflected in the curved glass of his aviators. A waitress, young, walks over. Josh tries to order for the two of them in Chinese; he mangles it, but she likes the effort and giggles down at him.

"Very good," she says.

"I'm a linguist," he says.

She walks away, and Josh says she has a pretty nice rack for a Chinese girl. Dan agrees. Josh leans back, his left arm stretched across the empty chair next to him. Dan imagines Josh's mouth on the waitress's nipples, sucking, the sound that would make.

"Depp is the man," Josh says.

21 Jump Street has sort of become their thing. *21 Jump Street* on Thursday, a party on Friday, dim sum on Saturday morning to recap the conquests of the night before.

"*Freeze,*" Josh screams across the table, pointing a finger gun at Dan, face perfectly Depp-ish. "*Freeze.*"

Dan throws his hands up and tries to say, *Ah, c'mon man,* like a pimp just caught. They laugh together.

Josh has a girlfriend, a new one, and he starts talking about her. Her name is Naya, and she's Indian or Bangladeshi, Dan never gets it right. Sometimes she goes out with them on Fridays. She doesn't say much. Josh leaves her next to Dan, goes off somewhere to talk to other people, returns after too long. She asks Dan, *Where* is *he?* She loves him, loves him to the point of stinging tears and gnawing stomach pain when she can't see him. When Josh returns home after dim sum, Dan knows there will be messages on his mother's answering machine, aching messages. Josh will call Dan, say listen, and then hit Play, and Dan will hear him laughing into his protein shake as Naya's recorded voice whines, *Where are you?*, yet again, trying so hard to sound nonchalant, which makes it sound the opposite. *Are you screening? Pick up if you're there. Hello?*

"She fucks crazy," Josh says, leaning over the table. "These Indian girls, they're proper, they're not supposed to, so it's like they're dying for it."

Dan is silent as he tries to imagine what *dying for it* means, and what it might look like. He imagines the sound of struggling breath, hair yanked back, eyes wide in a perfect ratio of pleasure and pain. A few months ago, it had been another girl. At the same table over dim sum, Josh had told Dan all about her family, so overprotective that she'd been brainwashed away from sex until marriage. Which was bullshit. But Josh, the pull of him, his insistence, it was all too much. She agreed to anal as a compromise, whispered that in his ear, and then Josh relayed the message to Dan in more of a yell, talking about the *tightness* of it. All Dan could say was, *How tight? How tight?*

The waitress is standing over the front counter by the mints looking at their table.

"You like her?" Josh says.

"Well, yeah," Dan says.

"Do you want her?"

"Sure, but—"

"That's it. Shut up. I just asked you if you wanted her."

The moment slows down after this. Josh stands, winks, strides across the little restaurant. The waitress sees him coming and tries to pretend like she doesn't. Dan watches the distance between them close and feels the weight of inevitability. He doesn't hear any of the exchange. He sees Josh move in, lean over, and speak.

Josh returns with her name and number written on a blank ticket. He slides it to his friend, a gift, a kindness, and he gives a little bow.

The next time Dan sees him bow is for real, a bow to a roomful of people. The people are clapping and so he's bowing. He's on a professional stage for the first time. Not just any professional stage; this is CBGB, as real a setting for a rock star as exists in the world. Fucking CBGB, and he's being watched like this is a school bus on Roosevelt Island and everyone else is a twelve-year-old girl. It feels like a scene that Dan will remember as a beginning. He will be able to tell people, anybody, years from now, I was in the *first* crowd.

Josh is standing behind the keyboard that he taught himself to play. He doesn't look nervous and he doesn't look to anyone for validation. He looks down at his own fingers, and then out over the crowd at some point beyond. Dan sees him at an angle reserved for concert documentaries, lots of crotch and chin.

The club isn't full. It's a Wednesday, after all, and Josh is not Joe Strummer. Dan recognizes almost every person in the room. Josh's parents are in the front, beaming, his father clicking a newly bought camera like a zinc-faced whale watcher. Dave is in the back sulking into a soda. Friends are in the crowd, old classmates from Roosevelt Island who stand around Dan in a jealous pack, shy immigrant girls he's met at Josh's college parties. Yeah, you could see it like a talent-show crowd, and you could see how poorly that fits the surroundings—proud parents taking mantel photos in the place where Iggy Pop used to cut his skin to let fans lick his blood.

But Josh is backlit onstage, and he looks the part. There is a red glow coming from behind his neck. His body is pulsing with breath. His arms are like snakes snapping at the keys. His mouth is open and his eyes are closed as he sings a low harmony. Dan is standing as tall as he has ever stood, right in the middle of the front row, fists raised, metal buckles jangling on his leather jacket, howling at my brother engulfed in a spotlight as the first song begins its crescendo.

Static. Then the downfall.

Six years later, Dan's leather jacket is folded up tight and rests in a plastic box in a hall closet at his mother's apartment. The motorcycle that he bought with his first string of paychecks, that even Josh was jealous of, is packed up, too, covered in an old sheet. The bike makes his girlfriend nervous. She's a nurse and she has pulled metal shards out of bloody holes in a triage unit, so danger carries no awesomeness for her. She works all day, comes home with sore feet, and likes to lie on the couch with Dan in their starter apartment in Queens, with the news on, feeding each other lo mein.

Josh is in their apartment now for the first time, and just his presence, his insincere compliments about their taste in furniture, is making her nervous. Dan is busy staring at Josh's sweaty face, the ring of new flesh that submerges his once lean jawline. Dan is trying to remember what Josh's jaw used to look like. He wants to take his fingers and frame Josh's head, to cut out all the excess from the image and remind himself. Then he wants to put his girlfriend's face behind his finger frame and say, *See?*

He and Josh rarely see each other anymore. It's not like they had a fight; it's just that Dan began living this life, and Josh began living another one. Dan isn't exactly sure what that life is. For a while, he just assumed that Josh had finally found more interesting people to be around. Dan would call his apartment, and when Josh picked up, he sounded distracted, far away. He said, Dan, I'm working. Or, Dan, I'm writing. Then he mostly stopped picking up.

"Nice candles," Josh says to Dan's girlfriend, then smirks. "They smell great. What's that smell?"

"Autumn," she says.

They are silent after this. Dan wants to tell a story about the time he saw Josh onstage at CBGB playing the keyboard, then turn to his girlfriend and say, "You like music, right?" He wants to reconcile two lives. He wants to defend his home and his matching furniture and the woman that he bought it with. But more so, troublingly more so, he wants to defend Josh to her. It is a special loneliness to be flanked by two people who you love who do not like each other, an empty feeling to know that they don't see what you see.

Dan defends nobody and instead goes to piss, walking stiff and hurried out of the room like it's an emergency. For two minutes, he leaves his girlfriend alone on the couch next to Josh, leaning away from the slow breath and dilated eyes that she diagnosed the moment he walked in the door.

Dan returns ready to tell a story about middle school that is too boring to upset anyone, but Josh is at the door, putting his sneakers on and mumbling that he's late for something. Dan stammers out a noise, not a real word. Josh is already opening the door, then already gone. Dan's girlfriend is up, saying, "If he comes in here again, I'm leaving."

"Wait, why?"

She speaks fast. "He asked me to write him prescriptions and

I said I could lose my job for that, and then he asked again and I said please stop, but he wouldn't so I told him to get out."

Dan says, "What does he need a prescription for?"

She says, "Oh, Jesus, Daniel, really?"

In bed that night, she asks him what it is about Josh. What's worth caring for in a man like that? Dan stares up at the white ceiling, the fan moving in slow, shaking rotations. He remembers drumsticks and lockers and dim sum and women, each of them the most beautiful woman ever to live. He says nothing. She coaxes him, not in an accusing way, but gently. She wants to understand. He loves her. She says, "I don't get people like that. Who have everything and then screw it up. It doesn't make any sense." She's right, but Dan has never stopped to judge Josh and doesn't want to now. He wants to say something about Josh's humor and how he could lock his eyes on you, how that felt. He wants to say something about desire, too, about the intoxication of being around somebody who feels like he *deserves* all that he can think to desire. How easy it is to believe that. But everything Dan remembers feels small and shallow as he remembers it, and he thinks the memories might shrink even more if he says them out loud. He stays silent until they fall asleep.

Josh never returns to the apartment, but his voice does. He leaves so many messages on the answering machine in his last years. Dan comes home from work, hits the button, hears the beep, and then Josh's voice is in his living room. Dan's now fiancée stands behind him with her arms folded as he listens. *Danny Boy,* Josh begins like old times. *You there? Danny Boy, pick up. Dan? Buddy, where are you?*

First it's exciting. Then it's irritating. Then Dan feels himself beginning to dread his friend's voice because to hear it is to pity him, and he doesn't know how to pity Josh, doesn't want to learn.

He agrees to meet up just to make the phone calls stop. Josh gives him an address in Astoria, a few blocks from the 7-train, on a street full of closed auto repair shops. It's a basement apartment. A woman Dan has never met lets him in and says nothing to him. She isn't beautiful. Skin hangs off her as though she was born with extra. She folds in on herself as she walks.

She sits next to Josh. Dan sits on the edge of a kitchen chair and rubs his hands together for no reason. Josh doesn't move, but his eyes fix on Dan. He says that he's happy to see him. Then says it again.

"Danny Boy," he says. "I want to know about you. Tell me about you."

This might be the first time in their relationship that Josh has asked outright like that. Dan begins to talk, but stops as Josh grabs a rubber tube off the couch next to him and ties it tight around his biceps.

"I'm listening," he says, "Talk."

Dan speaks in quick syllables, only continues when Josh urges him on. He tells him that life is good. It's just life. Job, drinks on the weekends. Other stuff. It's all fine.

As he speaks, he watches Josh and the woman take turns injecting each other. At first, he wonders if this is for his benefit, Josh looking to surprise one last time. But it's not that; he's not looking for a reaction at all. He's just doing what needs doing. Dan watches Josh's fingers, still strong and graceful, as he feels for her vein like it's a note and then slips the needle in, presses down gently with his thumb until the brown stuff is all gone. Dan watches their heads loll back together. He watches their quick eye contact over the shared bliss and then watches their eyes dull into something painted.

Josh offers once; Dan declines. Josh shrugs. Then silence.

The silence extends for the better part of an hour. Dan keeps his eyes on his friend as he moves through strange pulses of life—sits up, snorts, giggles a little, then sinks back down. Dan looks at Josh's body melting into the scabbed skin of this woman who never told him her name. They breathe together until Dan can't figure out whose breath is whose. He tries to hold his own breath; he's not sure why. Two pigeons fight outside the window and their racket startles him. He listens to that for a while. He stands and debates whether to touch his friend's shoulder, but he doesn't want to feel how that must feel, because then he won't forget it. He walks out fast, shuts the door softly.

Static.

Small talk is difficult with Dan. He seems hell-bent on making it but has absolutely no aptitude for it. I'm on my third Pepsi because when he can't think of anything else to say he says, "You want a Pepsi or something? They're free. I'll go get you one."

"Thanks, man," I say when he hands them to me.

"Oh, don't worry about it," he says. "I told you it's not a problem *at all.*"

We're high up in a building somewhere in Midtown. We're in the office of a moderately sized hedge fund. Dan does computer stuff for them, which is why we're in here on a Saturday afternoon, alone.

"You know, you take a nine-month course and you're certified," he tells me. "It's an option. Everybody needs IT."

"Oh yeah, totally, thanks, I'm just bad at computers," I say.

"Yeah, it's not easy," he says.

He tells me he has an access key for work so he can get in the office anytime, because if something goes wrong, if all this money—and it's some important people's money—gets trapped in a system error, only he can save them from financial ruin. I am impressed by this, though less impressed than I act.

We're at a table meant to seat thirty men in striped suits, not just the two of us, miniature, me in my stubbornly childish jean-shorts and band T-shirt, Dan with a newish gut hanging over his waist, polo tucked snugly into weekend Dockers. He looks like an avid but horrible golfer, a man whose greatest pleasure is drunk-flirting with strangers at happy hour. That's not fair. But if you talk about another man's beauty for long enough and he's not around to provide a dose of reality, it makes those who remain alive seem even more mundane than they already are.

We're surrounded by windows, a whole building of windows, and across from these windows are other windowed buildings full of empty rooms like this one. I don't like it, the reflection of the same thing back at itself, over and over, no beginning or end. Dan tells me that sometimes, not often, he regrets not seeing Josh much in the last years. I ask him if he's haunted by those final memories, if they stay with him. He says no, nothing like that.

"Josh used to have this joke about me," he says. "He'd be, like, *Hey, if Dan came in and found you fucking his mom, what would he say? And the answer was, Hey, Ma, what's for dinner?*"

Dan laughs at this. It's funny because it's true, he says. He's a pretty mellow guy. Doesn't really like to dwell. And Josh was just crazy, man. Dan reiterates that. Josh could do anything and would do anything. He says each *anything* with this heavy, cartoony, eyebrow-arching quality, I think so that we can share in that sense of wide-eyed dirty talk.

This character, this break-room legend, is the opposite of the boy Philip Goodman remembers. At first, as Dan spoke of him, I felt relief, then goose-bumped curiosity. This was the brother I had wanted to see—bold, grinning, phallic. But now I'm uneasy. The forced glory was short-lived and Josh is still distant. Mostly I feel like we're laughing at his bad jokes.

Dan asks if I'm the same kind of guy as my brother.

"Not the whole, you know, drug addict part, but just being, you know, one of those people?" he says.

I consider lying, but it doesn't seem like a believable lie, so I say no.

"Figured," he says. "Most people aren't like that. Most people are like me. I got this feeling you were kind of like me."

This is so simplifying and stupid, yet so simultaneously true, that I can't get a handle on how to be offended by it. I nod at him.

He asks me things.

Do I have a girlfriend? Yes.

Do I love her? Yes.

Uh-oh. Marriage? Oh, well, I mean, who knows.

"It's not so bad," Dan tells me.

He gestures out, maybe to his wife in Queens, but also to everything around him in his universe. He describes his routines, breaks them down in hour chunks—the commute, the job, the mortgage, a kid, something about buying a grill. He speaks as though he is welcoming me into this, each segment of his life.

It's hard at this empty conference table not to dichotomize real-Dan and remembered-Josh into figureheads—two distinct models for how to grow into a man, with no room for subtlety between them. One did it with slow, unremarkable dedication, plodding progress that was hard for anyone to notice; and one achieved the alternative—he simply didn't do it at all. That's how Josh became a myth. Which can be great for a while—me and Dan laughing at the memories, talking about Josh being a crazy bastard with the kind of head-bobbing emphasis reserved for when the phrase *crazy bastard* is used by the uncrazy. A myth is so much better than a person, but as we repeat the myth again and again, different versions, closely scrutinized, the form doesn't hold. It's *too* inhuman.

My brother, Dan's friend, has become a series of predictable, if reassuring, patterns in our conversation. Even his death feels expected, a variation of burning out instead of fading away, that old line. I don't think Dan has ever mourned him, just mythologized. Maybe I've done the same.

Dan has to go, he tells me in the middle of another conversation about anal sex that neither of us had. Dinner. It's four p.m. But he has to get home and then shower. Friends are coming over, his wife's work friends. It's one of those dinners that will end up being a whole production. The kind where you almost forget to eat because there's so much to be done, you know? I say I don't know, not really, and he says I will.

We stand and shake hands like one of us just sold the other a car.

Josh, or his memory, the guy who felt nothing but freedom and bliss, then death, is the most interesting character either of us has ever known.

I interrupt Dan mid-story, waiting for the elevator. I want to clarify something.

"So, this was about twenty-two or twenty-three?" I say, trying to confirm the timing of one of Dan's memories.

"Oh, no, it was way more girls than that," he says.

I start to explain, but stop short.

"With all the stories I've got on that fucker, it's got to be way more," he says. "I mean, right? And that's just counting the regular girls, not even the whores. Did you know about that?"

He gives a short wince; then it's gone. I didn't know about that. I lie and tell him I did, so he grins.

"I told him, why pay? You can get any girl you want," Dan says. "And he told me, *Hey, it's cheaper than taking them out to dinner.* That's funny, huh? And pretty true."

I want to say something combative to give Dan an indication that we're not in on this last joke together. I want to tell him I don't believe him, but I'm not sure if that's true and I'm not sure if it changes anything anyway. Instead, I feed the myth. I hear myself blurting out a memory of my own, a last dirty anecdote for us to smirk at.

Josh took me to the Hard Rock Cafe in Times Square once. It was me and him and an Indian woman who made me blush every time she looked at me. And she brought along her little brother, too, who was my age. I think we were nine.

The boy and I became friends for the evening, staring with one unified gaze. We were old enough to want to know what our siblings did to each other. We were waiting for something to happen. Josh's knuckles brushed her arm. She laughed. He smiled. I liked the accent that she spoke with, how her mouth formed so wide and circular around her vowels when she responded to him, like everything Josh said was a surprise. There was a shining stud in her left nostril, and I kept looking at it, thinking how much it must hurt to pierce your face.

Josh beat out a rhythm on our table, and I watched the ice in my Coke bob in the current he created. He whispered something to her that made her smile. Her teeth were white like they'd been painted.

They left us. Josh's hand found her back pocket as they walked, and I watched the outline of his fingers in tight denim. My new friend and I giggled.

Time was slow for us. We waited for our siblings until we couldn't wait anymore. The boy raised his eyebrows at me, thick eyebrows on a small face. I remember the hot blush on my cheeks as we crept toward the bathrooms, past signed head shots and V-shaped guitars, past a waitress crouching carefully in a miniskirt to tie her shoes.

They were in the handicapped bathroom. We didn't see but we heard.

It was breath, mostly. Her exhalations were like strands of music, reaching us under the crack of the closed door. There was something like a growl from Josh. I wondered if I would ever make such a noise, what it would take to produce it.

Oh shit, oh shit, in his voice, and I held my hand over my mouth to shove laughter back in. Her voice wasn't profane, just overwhelmed. *Oh, oh, oh, oh.*

"That's awesome," Dan says when I'm done. "I bet I could figure out who that girl was for you. No, sorry, not now. Dinner. Sorry. Man, I could do this all day."

He shrugs and offers me another Pepsi for the road, but I say no, too much sugar. I hold my gut, jiggle it. He says, Don't I know it? Then there's another handshake, the last one, and the vague promise of doing this again over beers. Dan is smiling as the elevator door closes.

Josh never wrote his erotic legends. He never described a flirtation, a date, an orgasm. He never described the feeling of standing on a stage or the buzz of a party where he was the star. The tone of my talk with Dan, the details he gave me—it all fades almost instantly against what Josh left behind. He deemed nothing Dan remembers worth recording. There are women's names, yes, references to rage and regret, the ways that they hurt him and the ways he planned to hurt them back. But he never recorded the routine glory that he described to his friend. Either it wasn't important or he was ashamed or he was lying.

The closest thing I find to sex writing is a poem that's more about intimacy, that thing that Dan and I never really got to see:

[POEM, UNDATED, "THE LITTLE GIRL"]:
Little girl
Who looked up at me

Knowing nothing.
Oh underdog triumph

I am you! I swim in you,
Never wanting to break free of your awkwardness.

I live my life as the hunter,
But I am also hunted.
Like you little girl.
Like you.

One day we'll mesh.
Not prosaic lust
But real love.
Love is understanding.
Love is doing back to you.
Because you will never leave.

Feel me, what little there really is.
I will be there as the hermit, as the warrior.
And you will teach me magnificence.

. . .

When Josh died, I focused my thoughts on his snake. Because when I thought of him, I thought of danger and fear and power and appetite and joy. I thought of those things all swirled together, impossible to distinguish, and it was too much, too fraught, so I shut off the complexities and just remembered the snake.

The snake was named Percy. Percy was a boa constrictor and Percy was eight feet long and Percy could kill a grown man in four minutes. I remembered the frantic questions in my head as a little boy—*I'm not even a grown man, so how fast could Percy kill me?* I remembered being seven, eight maybe, when Josh held up a tube of toothpaste with no toothpaste left in it. He said that's what your body would look like if Percy held you tight. I thought of the pressure making my head pop open, my mouth a hinge. I thought of my intestines squirting out, a green-and-white spearmint froth.

There were little scenes that I focused on in memory. Not even scenes so much as images that would reoccur, always in Josh's apartment, just the two of us and Percy. Josh kept the lights low so Percy could sneak up on you. One time, Percy wrapped himself around the pull-up bar by the front door. He dropped his face down in front of mine and his eyes were gray, I think. I screamed and Josh laughed and Percy slid onto him, curled himself around my brother's shoulders.

Josh looked happy with the snake on him, so I was happy, too. I pet the snake's scales and we went to watch TV.

It was Percy's fault when I wasn't allowed back into Josh's apartment. There was a specific moment that I used most to explain his steady removal from my life. My mother came to pick me up from Josh's, and Percy was wrapped two times around my waist. We'd been watching a Rambo movie and taking turns holding the snake, pretending he was a belt of ammunition. My mother walked in and found me splaying my legs, holding one hand against my hip like an action figure, one hand gripping Percy. I laughed and Josh laughed, but she didn't, and I thought maybe that was because Percy was so tight on me and she could see my soft stomach indent every time he breathed.

Josh's speech was slow and slurred, which I knew, but didn't really know.

"Are you scared?" he asked me.

I said no, of course.

"Good, you shouldn't be scared of things," he said to me.

"See, he's not scared," he said to my mother.

She reached out for my hand, and he threw his arm heavy across my shoulders, and Percy kept his grip around my stomach.

Josh said, "We're just two guys and a snake," and I laughed at that. My mother did not.

I got an iguana for my ninth birthday because I wanted something cold and prehistoric, like what Josh had. My iguana was a compromise. He had no teeth. He was safe and mostly I hated him. We fed him banana slices and he couldn't hold them in his mouth. He jerked his head around, epileptic. He ran in place on polished wood floors because he couldn't get traction. He was useless, but he kept on living, and later, when I wasn't allowed back into Josh's apartment, I'd watch my iguana sit perfectly still and I'd pine for the snake.

The last night I slept at Josh's, we watched *Godzilla* in the dark. I lay across his chest and his heart beat slow and heavy.

He said, "Look at those little pussies," and he pointed to the Tokyo citizens screaming in black-and-white on-screen. He pulled his eyes slanty and said, *Oh, no, me so scared!* So I did, too. We laughed at the Japanese for being so frightened of a monster, as Percy slid silently across the TV console. Josh fell asleep, and I kept my head on his chest.

In the morning, we dangled white mice over Percy's tank. Josh dropped his in, and it paced in panicked circles until it seemed to resign itself to what was coming and leaned its body against the glass to wait. He dared me to drop mine in, so I did, and then yanked my hand back as though there would be an instant repercussion. We didn't watch the squeezing or the eating, although in the story I would tell at school, the squeezing was brutal and awesome, little mouse eyes popping out and sticking to the glass. Percy was the size of a fire-truck hose in my story, and he had fangs.

When I was eleven, we left my iguana with Josh and went away on vacation. The iguana never came home. The claim was natural causes, but I wasn't fooled. The iguana had gone to a place that was far too great for him to survive; I should have anticipated this. Josh called and the phone was passed to me. He said he wished there was something he could have done; the little guy just stopped breathing in the middle of the night. It had always been a fragile creature, he reminded me. I agreed, yeah, totally, a pitiful thing.

"When you're sad, listen to 'Dear Prudence,'" he told me, and then he hummed a bit and I liked the sound. "It's about how Mia Farrow's sister is too scared to have fun, but she shouldn't be."

I wasn't sure who Mia Farrow was, but I said okay.

My parents treated me with special, restrained care for a week or so because I'd lost my faithful companion, which felt ridiculous and embarrassing. I was talked to gently, but gently never made it better. I wanted to feel the bad things. I wanted to see the body. I imagined the outline of my iguana's face fossilized, pressing against Percy's stomach. I imagined blood on leather. I wanted to be worthy of witnessing a casual death, quick and vicious.

I don't think anybody ever knew what happened to Percy. As the needle became more constant and obvious, Percy seemed of little consequence to my parents when they talked in hushed tones about Josh's apartment. An eight-foot-long muscle, he was comparably benign, and that made me angry because, hello, there's a snake, a dinosaur, a man-eater just slithering around the kitchen and everyone wants to whisper about something *else*? I felt bad for Percy then, his magnitude no longer respected. Sometimes, when Josh was discussed over dinner, I'd interject.

"How's Percy?" I would ask.

"What?"

"He means the snake."

"The snake is a snake. The snake is fine."

Percy stopped being altogether at some point before Josh did. I'm pretty sure I just assumed that because he wasn't mentioned when my father returned from the scene of his son's death, whispered to my mother that the body was cold. So I figured the paramedics didn't complain of a monster dropping on them from a pull-up bar when they entered the apartment. I thought of my brother's home devoid of Percy, his slow slither, his constant, alive threat, and that's when the grief felt actual.

Percy must have starved for a long time before he finally died because boa constrictors do not die as easily as people do. I thought about that often in the first months post-Josh. When it was just me and my father in the house, nobody talking, I thought about Percy starving and never brought it up. I thought about how Josh must have become tempting to his snake, a year's worth of nourishment and almost too easy. I thought of Percy curled atop the TV console, watching, hungry. I thought of Josh's face fossilized against Percy's scales like a dead iguana, and how massive a lump he would have been inside that body. I let it feel like there was choice, respect even, in that snake's decision not to eat that man. Josh had tamed him and he remained unafraid for as long as he remained. That was an important thing to think.

I became afraid of everything. I slunk toward extreme self-preservation. I waited like a tourist for the light to change before venturing into the street. Sometimes I stood still and looked both ways until the light changed back. Weekends were frightening, all that time and expectation. I fled from friends and novice parties filled with harmless indiscretion, giving stories about a strict curfew that did not exist. I begged my father to call parent-free apartments and demand, with believable drama, that I return home at once. I liked to sit alone and watch movies. I liked to fall asleep. I got an acoustic guitar and I tried my hand at writing songs the way Josh wrote songs, but all of my songs were about not leaving the house or they were about him, the mystery of the things he did, Percy wrapped around his shoulders in the dark.

There was a tattoo parlor down the street, run by two guys

with earrings so big that goldfish lived inside them. They had a Komodo dragon as the store pet. On hot days, they let the dragon sit in a kiddy pool on the sidewalk, and they strolled him up and down the block on a dog's leash. Sometimes they let me walk the dragon, and I allowed myself that indulgence. I thought of Josh when I felt the looks of passersby as the dragon pulled the leash tight. I reached down to pet its scales, and I liked the way they felt against my palm.

At a dinner party full of my parents' friends, Sofia is telling a story she heard about a woman and her pet snake. And so of course I'm thinking about Percy and his scales. She's a good storyteller and she's reaching the dramatic climax—a vet tells the woman that her snake sleeps next to her like that because he's sizing her up, seeing if she could fit in him once he unhinges his jaw. The whole time she thought he was bonding, but he was plotting. Dinner party attendees are squealing.

One friend of my mother's says, "No. *No.* That did *not* happen," which may be true.

I think we got to this story because people were doing the cats-versus-dogs argument and then the idea of which animals really care about you, really *connect* with you, came up, so somebody started talking about weird pets, the kind that can't love at all, and then Sofia jumped in with the snake anecdote.

I'm proud of her when she finishes. This is a room full of near strangers for her, and she's charmed them, which I think is a positive reflection on me. I like hearing her tell stories, but sometimes I feel nervous as she starts them. I look around at whatever group we're in and worry about the humor missing, until somebody laughs, and then everyone does, and I feel the gentle slackening of relief.

She likes snakes. She has a snake tattoo that curves around her left hip and heads toward her ribs. She got it on her eighteenth birthday. She says she regrets it but I don't believe her. Once, when an exotic petting zoo set up in a parking lot at our college, she let the carny teach her how to milk viper's venom. She let him put a boa constrictor around her shoulders. She held her arms out, did a weird Christlike or Britney Spears–like snake pose, and some of our friends took pictures for Facebook. The carny was so impressed he gave a pervy whistle. He said, Man, chicks *never* do that. I was proud and terrified and then, later, jealous when we lay on her dorm bed and she said there was something cool, like primordial cool, about a man handling a snake. I got flushed and she said stop and I said, "Stop what? I'm not even doing anything."

I got up and looked down on her with what I hoped was calm derision.

I said, "There is nothing lamer than dudes who own snakes. You might as well think magicians are cool."

I hated it the moment I said it. It felt like a confession. If Josh walked into our dorm right then, snake-draped, in his leather jacket and aviators, looking for my or anyone's girlfriend, I would have thought him insufferable.

I am very afraid of snakes now. I don't like the way they feel, just armored muscle.

After the dinner party, we're in bed talking. Sofia is worried.

She says, "Do you think it was too weird a story?"

I say, "No, they loved it, it was memorable. People remember stuff like that."

"Too memorable?"

"No, the right amount of memorable. Everybody loved you."

She closes her eyes and I kiss her eyelids. She smiles and says she likes when I do that. Then we are quiet together.

We live on the sixth floor of a turreted prewar building off

Flatbush Avenue, far away from anyone we know. In my father's generation, Jewish immigrants lived in this neighborhood. Now it's nearly all black, having gone through that most common New York evolution. We call it the frontier of gentrification out here, though that waifish blonde always wheeling her harp into the elevator suggests that we aren't the first settlers. On Sunday mornings, I like to leave our windows open and listen to the microphoned preacher of the Haitian Tabernacle Church next door, a detail of our lives that gives me an unreasonable amount of joy, just the idea that I am a grown man finding my way in a world so gritty that it includes patois.

My father grew up in Coney Island, the son of a cab driver with a gambling addiction. He read a lot, ran the bumper cars at the theme park, never gambled, and hated Brooklyn. Josh was a little boy in Sheepshead Bay, right next to Coney Island, overlooking the Atlantic, and the family moved to Roosevelt Island when his father got a good job in advertising and became more of the man he wanted to be. Still, Josh grew up viewing Manhattan from across a river. I was born downtown, never knew a life not surrounded by the place people want to live and the things people want to own.

Yet *this* is the place I want. It's the opposite of Josh's fantasies, but I'm proud of this roach-infested monument to semi-independence, with its rent-controlled grandmother neighbors and dollar stores, the smell of salt fish on the street. I've fled to Brooklyn with an eye for romance the way my father once fled from it. It's the current of how generations live in this place.

As I try to conceive of my life, the potential development of it, I see Josh's stunted life and our father's long life in sheets of clear tracing paper stacked over one another, different lines on the same city grid. Josh's lines move in reaction to our father's steady, straight success. Then my sheet settles on top of both of theirs, my line tiptoeing around the places and movements they've already claimed, unsure.

Sometimes it seems like the paths that they walked, that I am walking, were preordained, or at least entirely circumstantial. So when I search for Josh's *reasons*, unique and explainable qualities that made him push too far, all I find are the cue cards for every pampered white boy flailing around trying to be a man in the nineties. He came of age in the earnest, self-affirmational eighties. Then he lived in Murray Hill, downtown, surrounded by up-and-coming Wall Street plug-ins, in an apartment that his dad paid for, with a black leather couch like you see in high-class porn. Then, when the soon-to-be-a-star narrative ran out, he was just a guy with artsy inclinations and nonspecific business cards, and all of a sudden it was the mid-nineties and there were needles lying on park benches when he walked out for bodega coffee. That was never my world. I can't know what I'd have done differently if it had been.

The next night, Sofia and I walk to a party in Bedford-Stuyvesant at a renovated brownstone that houses five of our friends. We find someone who has coke and try to beg in a dignified way for a line. A small group of us goes into a bedroom and we snort. We play ironic techno music about shopping and dance around with one another. We are all, really all of us, wearing plaid shirts, bought used, the kind Josh wore to cover track marks when everyone else did that, too. We laugh a lot. We plan a group trip to Virginia Beach for New Year's, because who goes to Virginia Beach in the winter?

This is strong coke, and soon I feel my body tighten, picture my blood as a fist, punching at the limits of my veins. I feel a ghost hand on my neck.

I'm asked, "What's wrong?"

I say, "Nothing."

I stand alone by the door. It's midnight, still early. Sofia walks over, presses herself into my body. She smells like cigarettes. She says, "I'm tired, take me home."

I want to go, too, but I feel that I shouldn't.

"Come on, let's stay," I say. "You're the only person who gets tired on coke."

"I'll leave alone, then," she says.

She knows I won't let that happen, and she waits by the door for me to grab my jacket and follow. On the street, in the cold, she apologizes and says I didn't have to leave. I say, It's fine, in a passive-aggressive way. But it *is* fine. I never stay. I never push. And I like that she can play the foil, while I pretend that all I want to do is linger, that I dull my true inherited nature out of consideration for her.

We walk home, a bit frightened in this neighborhood so late at night. My arm is around her and I'm reveling in the impulse to protect. We walk past more buildings, look into more windows, imagine. We ask each other questions: If we could live anywhere, where? If it's a choice between a patio and a bay window, which do we have to have? I try to push the conversation to what might happen tonight, in our bedroom, things we've never tried. She stops, grabs my shoulder, and says, "Should we have bought some? Just for us to have? We could stay up all night. It would be fun, right?"

I tell her it's better that we didn't. I say I'm still a little buzzed anyway, which I'm pretty sure is a lie. She agrees and we keep walking, content to explain to each other all the ways that we think we feel a little different than normal. At home, we drink water, take Advil, fall asleep.

The next morning, I wake up early and make us eggs. I spoon them onto her plate and have a flash of memory: Percy on the pull-up bar after Josh finished a set; Josh cracking raw eggs into protein powder, shaking, drinking.

Sofia says, "Will you be insulted if I put salt on these?"

I say, "No, I mean, I already salted them, so they shouldn't need any, but go ahead."

When we're done eating, we clean the turtle tank. Last year, Sofia bought a turtle and named her Heidi, so now we have to care for her. Heidi lives in an overpriced aquarium next to the TV. Mostly, she sleeps on a rock under a lamp, but every month or so her water gets putrid brown and we have to set her on the bathroom floor while we dump her filth out in the tub.

"Watch her," Sofia says, straddling the tank, scrubbing the glass with rubber gloves. "Don't let her run away."

The turtle hasn't moved. She's settled under the radiator for warmth.

"She's not going anywhere," I say.

"Well, she's scared, poor thing," Sofia says. "Hold her."

Suddenly, I am enraged. I start yelling.

"I hate that fucking turtle," I yell. "It doesn't *do* anything. Why the fuck do we keep it alive?"

Sofia calls me an asshole. I stomp out of the bathroom and she finishes alone. She lugs the clean tank back into the living room, sets it down on the table next to the TV, then glares at me. I pretend to be reading. The church starts up next door. I hear the shaky hum of chords on an electric keyboard. She places Heidi back on the rock, under the lamp, and Heidi doesn't move. Sofia sits down on the couch next to me, and I apologize without specifics. She pulls a fleece blanket over both of us. We sit and listen to the electric keyboard, and I run my fingers along her neck, careful not to squeeze. We watch the turtle.

"Do you think she's warm enough?" Sofia says. "I hope she's warm."

———

Josh recognized the power of his snake as a metaphor. He got Percy before he got high, but he soon made the connection—those forces that he kept closest to him, that held him tight.

He left behind long, free-associative journals from each time he tried to get clean. They were meant for revisiting, full of little annotations and Post-it-note reminders: *Read this when it gets hard! Learn!* Now I force myself to revisit them, because it's in these journals that he seems at his most bluster-less. And in so many of them, through dreams and memories and promises, a serpent slithers.

[NOTEBOOK, UNDATED, "DETOX JOURNAL"]:

It seems that my life has been a mental struggle. An aggregate of the madness (panic attacks), fear of sleep (real fear!), fear of darkness, pathological shyness toward girls from ages 14–19. Since I was conscious, cognizant of the world, it has been a mental struggle.

Paxil is a gift from the Heavens. No more panic attacks. But I still felt short changed. I always tried to like inebriates, but I either didn't like them or they made things worse. Pot, coke, alcohol, speed, and a plethora of prescription drugs did nothing. That's when I met the giant python.

She first came in the form of Percodan and Vicodin. She was still not squeezing me, but she looked so beautiful. I was petting her and she was writhing, ever so gently, around my limbs. I am not stupid. I know the dangers of a giant snake. But after all I had been through, I deserved it. I had been to hell. I was in purgatory. And for what? To be on anti-depressants so that I could be content? Fuck that. I deserved happiness. It was owed to me. The Serpent, she made me happy. She was beautiful. She still is.

She was tightening around me. I didn't care. Life went
from panic, to contentedness to bliss to euphoria. I was being
constricted.

I try to break free. She has grown. Oh, she has grown. While she
was on me, right under my nose, she grew. She knows what I like.
Knows what I need. And what I fear. I am being constricted.

It has always been so important for me to see Josh as fear-
less. To see the snake as another monster that he toyed with and
could control, at least for a while. It's harder to think about him
helpless and realizing it. To know that before the snake, before
the high, there was fear, and that being wrapped in something,
constricted, crushed, helped make the fear go away.

Later in the same journal, he writes immediately upon waking from a nightmare. He says he dreamed that he scored on East
Houston Street, by the river. He was frightened and confused,
didn't know how he got to where he was. He was surrounded
by prostitutes, all of them with "black girl" hair extensions. And
then he saw that some of the prostitutes were little children.
And then he was a little child, too. And then he saw a child's
skull with a snake weaving in and out of the eye sockets. He
didn't make it back home; he just stopped right there on Houston
Street, snorted the whole bag, and then woke up.

I have no idea if this has any meaning, but I can't stop thinking about him seeing himself as a child, lingering in the dark
places, using. He was a child and he was a corpse. The snake was
there from the beginning to the end.

The image pushes back against my memories. I was always a
child. He never was. I was dwarfed, afraid. He wasn't.

I still want to know more about what he felt, but each time
I lose a little obliviousness I long to take it back. I lay my head
across Sofia's lap on the couch, like I do sometimes. She pulls the

blanket up onto my shoulders. I watch the turtle stick her neck out, hit her nose on the glass, then snap back into her shell. I am so easily young again, looking up, waiting for something new to happen, trying to remember how it felt to be wrapped in his snake.

. . .

At seven years old, Caleb sits next to his aunt Beth and kicks his feet over the edge of floral-print couch cushions. He's watching cartoons and drinking orange juice, overcome by that special kind of obliviousness that children develop when faced with screens and straws.

"Are you hungry?" Beth is saying. "Hon, are you hungry?"

Caleb is oblivious, so he says nothing.

"You want some crackers? Some Oreos? You look hungry. I'm going to get you a plate of Oreos."

Caleb doesn't notice her leave his side and doesn't feel as exposed as maybe he should, because while he watches and sucks he doesn't see the planning of his abduction. He doesn't see Josh in the doorway giving a signal to Dave and Joey, Caleb's older brother. He doesn't hear Josh whisper, *Now.* He only registers the feeling of hands on him, grabbing his arms and legs, and then the sour taste of an extraordinarily pungent tube sock being shoved in his mouth. He struggles. He kicks a little, tries to yell, feels his own spit gurgling into the sock, mixing with someone else's sweat. Caleb is trussed up by his kin, Dave squeezing his ankles and Joey his wrists. He feels like one of the ducks in the window of the Chinese restaurant they go to on Christmas. He is dragged down the hall, and the gray carpet leaves sharp raspberries on his soft flesh. The stinging makes him want to cry, but he wills himself against that embarrassment.

He sees Josh, the mastermind, walking alongside him, grinning. It's a look of mischief and kindness all at once, and Caleb likes the layers of that. The smile promises torture, but it also commends Caleb, almost sweetly, for his willingness to take it. Josh winks. Or Caleb thinks he does. Yes, it was a wink. *Remember the wink,* he tells himself.

Caleb watches Josh run ahead into his bedroom to prepare.

"Bring him in," he orders from the top bunk. "Bring him in and let me get a look at him."

Caleb knows that Josh is doing an impression of Brando's voice in *The Godfather.* He doesn't know the original voice, only Josh's version, so he thinks the impression is flawless. He sits on the floor and feels many things. He is aware of how many things he is feeling, and that awareness is yet another feeling, awe at the overwhelming, near-physical presence of his emotion. He is terrified but joyous, breathless and panicked but easing into a sense of routine. He protests whatever may soon happen, but he hears laughter in his muffled pleas and realizes that he doesn't know if he's being sincere when he tries to beg for this to end.

Eventually, he exhausts himself. Josh grabs some rope from somewhere.

When Caleb is fully hog-tied, Josh counts punishment options on his fingers. He lets each threat linger on his tongue. He sits up straight and swells himself with breath. Caleb watches Josh's chest as it inflates and thinks about what his puny fist would sound like beating against that chest, and then thinks about an iron door-knocker echoing through a stone castle in an episode of *Scooby-Doo.* The air feels coated in potential. Caleb will soon be the vessel for something epic, and he knows it. There will be no common noogies or purple nurples. Not today, not here, not with Josh. This is a space of transcendent torture.

Caleb scrolls through options in his mind. Will it be the atomic wedgie, that perfectly symmetrical ass-chafing, a pair of hands on either side of his waist, yanking up so that the elastic of his tighty-whiteys grazes his ribs, then rocking him back and forth along that narrow balance beam of fabric until he bleeds and his kin claim that he's on his period, none of them quite sure yet what that means? Will it be the Punishment Dice, a term Josh coined, Caleb's fate decided by a roll—one promising a punch in the stomach, two a triple fart in the face, and so on, until heaven help you if you see a six? Will they hold his head in the bathtub again, make him trust that they won't let him drown?

Josh's smile grows, his teeth sharp, his cheeks ripping apart with happiness.

"Fuck it," he says, and Caleb's body shudders at the word. "Fuck it. It's summer. It's hot out. Let's get European. Strip him naked, boys."

They have to untie him first. The rope proves to be a totally pointless embellishment, but at least it makes the afternoon last. They tug at their inexpert knots until Caleb is finally free, but before he can run Josh grabs him. Caleb's shirt is ripped and then it's on the floor. Joey grabs the bottom of his jean shorts and lets Caleb's own futile struggles pull them down. Then each ankle sock comes off, even as he kicks and laughs because of the ticklish soles of his feet.

Finally, Caleb stands in just his underwear, Batman in five poses on his crotch, ready to fight. He tries to back away until there's no more space and he's pressed against Josh's dresser. There is a pause for effect. Josh steps forward and does an impression of a falsely well-intentioned father.

"Young man," he says. "You'll thank me for this someday."

As everyone laughs, Josh lunges and gives a quick yank. The underpants come down and then there it is—dangling little-boy penis, cold and pale.

"*Look* at it," Dave screams. He and Joey begin to flick at it, aiming to hurt.

How long? Caleb wonders, feeling the sting. *How long like this to make Josh happy?*

He will accept this treatment as long as he needs to, partly out of a lack of choice, partly because Josh's happiness makes Caleb feel like a new person, larger, buoyant. He will, he tells himself, stand naked and stinging in service of that feeling. But standing naked isn't enough. Josh is digging under his mattress. He exhumes a roll of duct tape, stolen from his mother days ago in the preplanning brainstorm phase. Dave and Joey emit owl hoots like a sitcom laugh track. Josh eyes his desk chair, that swiveling, wheeled, newly threatening contraption.

It's hard to know how much time is passing. Being with Josh feels like days when you're in the experience; then when the experience is taken away and you return to your small self alone, it feels like you only got seconds. Time is a banana slice trapped in a Jell-O mold as Caleb is strapped to the chair with circles of tape until every inch is used up, because, Josh says, safety first. Even his mouth is taped.

He hears his own heavy breath bursting out of his nose as he looks up at Josh wheeling the chair, hair flying off his ears as he breaks into a run down the hall toward the elevator. The door opens and Caleb feels himself spun and jostled as Josh wheels him right into the center of the elevator, facing forward so if you entered and happened to be looking down, you'd see all of Caleb's circumcised, prepubescent secrets. It's just the two of them for a moment. Josh whispers to him that he is a goddamn champion for doing this, and Caleb says, "Doing what?" But into the tape it sounds like nothing. Caleb looks up at Josh in the doorway. Josh gives a last grin, presses the button for every floor, all twenty, including the roof and the basement, and then exits.

Caleb rides the building alone. It seems that every elderly woman in the co-op has picked this exact time to go to the store. They scream and point their crooked old fingers at him and say, *Young man, what on* earth *do you think you're doing?* One lady just starts shrieking, no words. Eventually, Caleb gives in to the reckless hilarity of his situation. He has never felt like this before, unafraid of potential repercussions, immune to the size and the meanness of all the strangers in the world. He begins to laugh. Down and up, as the door opens at each floor, he is still cackling into tape, a screechy sound like a seagull.

He thinks of Josh. He thinks of him standing in the hallway on the fourteenth floor, laughing until his stomach hurts and he's gasping for air, falling down and laughing more. They are laughing at the same time, with the same feeling, with the same wildness in their eyes. Caleb is sure of it. He lets himself think that all of this has been an initiation into a way of being beyond boredom. And even if it isn't all that, it's still funny, so either way, success. And when finally the door opens back on the fourteenth floor, Josh is there just how Caleb imagined he would be, doubled over, laughter somehow shrill and bellowing all at once. Caleb has *predicted* this—what a sensation to feel. He has pictured his cousin in his mind and known him well enough for that mental image to conjure truth. Caleb hears his own laughter mix with Josh's, the tones rounding each other out, and he doesn't even flinch or yip as Josh yanks the tape off him and his blotched red skin snaps back into place. Caleb is happy, and pain, he thinks, right now and always, loses out to joy.

Joy and only joy. Joy on loop. Joy like an old cartoon chase where cat and mouse run through the same set the whole time. Joy like a game of free association—hear Josh's name and blurt out the word; hear the word and blurt out the name.

Caleb remembers joy.

"Maybe I'm disappointing you," he tells me. "But this is where I end."

It's not exactly true. We've been talking for a long time, weaving in and out of decades' worth of stories. He's told me about a beach scene when Josh swam, naked—I knew it even before Caleb said it—to capsize a day-sailer. Caleb watched from the boat as Josh's lithe teen body bobbed in and out of black water.

And there was a lovingly described tableau of Josh inconsolable right after John Lennon died. Caleb watched him as he listened to "Dear Prudence" on his bedroom floor, in awe of the magnitude of his grief, how much music could mean to a person.

There were assertions. Josh was smart, like crazy smart. In college, he gave Caleb philosophy books to read and Caleb got smarter just trying to do an impression of Josh's smartness. Heidegger, Nietzsche, Kant, all that shit. Josh really *got* it; Caleb just pretended, mostly.

He taught himself to play the piano—did I know that already?

He used to ride Rollerblades around the city as a teenager, hold on to the backs of trucks and go hurtling through rush-hour traffic. Never cared about a crash.

He had a big penis. Objectively.

Caleb has told me plenty, but we've returned to the first scene each time—how it feels to be young and helpless and taped nude to a chair.

I like Caleb. He's smart and has a sneaky, wry sense of humor. He laughs a lot and it's infectious.

We're in a law office, his law office, high above downtown Brooklyn. It's the end of his workday. There is rush-hour honking outside. Somebody calls somebody else a motherfucker down on the street, and we both hear it. Caleb says, "Might have a new personal injury client in a few minutes," and we both laugh. Caleb lets his laugh run out after a while, so I do, too. He's finishing his lunch at dinnertime at his desk. It smells like Russian dressing. He spills a little dressing on his tie, dabs.

I have been pushing him to remember differently, or more pointedly, with a little variety at least. He's tired and not interested in what I want.

He finishes his sandwich, then finishes his Diet Coke, then wipes his fingers on a paper napkin.

He says, "Look, I don't think of the addict part of Josh. It's separate. Whatever he became, that was somebody else. He's still a god to me."

"A *god*?" I say.

He says, "Oh, Jesus, it's not that deep. I remember him how he was."

But how *was* he? That's what I want to know. What is it that Caleb is so sure about? What's the recipe here? One part older cousin, one part violence, two parts inappropriate nudity, a sweet dash of kindness at the end, and then shake for the perfect manifestation of a preteen destined for great things? Caleb is looking at me, and underneath his smile I think I see strain—he doesn't want to say more than he's said.

He is physically small. His body would make sense on a child or an old man. Of all the men in his life who dwarfed him, the ones he loved most died, each in some way by his own hand. His youngest uncle killed himself with a bottle of Vicodin after years of taking just the right amount of Vicodin to not die. Joey, his older brother, had a heart attack a couple of years ago after a decade of on-and-off crack abuse. And then Josh. They were all, when Caleb remembers them, as large and beautiful and inevitable as shadows. There were so many things that they did, so many options that they had—smart, good-looking men who were loved, who people expected things from, not with a sense of pressure but a sense of assurance. Born protagonists.

Caleb has always felt secondary, but he is here. He is talking to me. None of the half men he loved managed that, and I ask him if he resents the fact that they deserted him. If he wanted so badly to be them, didn't they have a little responsibility to, you know, *be*? It shouldn't have been that hard for Josh to stay alive. If he could do *anything*, how come he couldn't do this one most basic thing? It's a rhetorical question, directed as much to me as it is to Caleb. When I hear myself say it, it sounds so hollow and obvious.

"It's not like that," Caleb says. "He just . . . he could have been a rock star so easily. Some kind of star. The kind of person people look at."

"Yeah, but he wasn't."

"Yeah, but he could have been."

In almost every memory I have of Josh, he's wearing a leather jacket. I think I've tampered with a good deal of the memories, since many of them are inside or on warm days when everyone else is wearing a T-shirt. Some are of me curled up against his body on the couch, watching old movies, the feel of cold sleeve studs on my cheek.

When Josh died, I got the jacket. Wherever I've moved, it's hung in the corner of my closet. It has no place in my real life; I favor comfort-fit Banana Republic denim and am not Billy Idol. But I wear it sometimes, always in performance. I wore it on Halloween in high school, when I didn't have a costume and was scrounging my room for something absurd. I brought it to college and wore it again on Halloween, and then to another costume party, complete with one of those combs made to look like a switchblade. And once to a Brooklyn birthday because the ironic Evite said, "Dress like you're ready to bash someone's face in, bro." And sometimes in the mirror, performing for myself.

There's always tension, because in the moment, on me, the jacket is so absurd, but it seems crucial that I retain nostalgia for the idea of it as a talisman of my brother. It covered Josh with metal scales, made photographers stop him on the street, made him smell like a cowboy and a greaser and a poet, and that's what he was. There was so much artifice to him. He didn't want to relate; he wanted to be ogled.

When addicts recover and live, I think part of the appeal of the story is that they've been stripped of artifice and they mature as humbled, extra-honest people. Humbling is always nice to observe. They speak quietly, with both nostalgia and remorse, about their past performances. They admit everything and make rueful, self-deprecating jokes that aren't meant to be laughed at. Josh died mid-performance, when I was still a child, when Caleb still experienced him as one.

Virginia Woolf described her earliest memories like this: *Many bright colours; many distinct sounds; some human beings, caricatures; comic; several violent moments of being, always including a circle of the scene which they cut out: and all surrounded by a vast space—that is a rough visual description of childhood.*

For Caleb and me, Josh is the bright color; he is the sound. He is that enormous caricature of what a human might be. He is the violent moment of being. And then there is vast space.

Woolf's mother died when she was thirteen.

I should be able to see her completely undisturbed by later impressions, she writes. But she can't. She remembers her mother's voice, her hands, the last exhalations of her laughter, the bracelets she wore and the sound they made when she moved, her beauty and how easy it was to accept that she was beautiful. She remembers quick scenes and bits of dialogue, but so much else is context—wanting it, not having it, adopting others'.

I see myself as a fish in a stream, she writes. *Deflected; held in place; but cannot describe the stream.*

There is too much hubris in this connection, but I do feel the stream, and it is hard to describe as it moves, and that is frustrating. And it's particularly frustrating when writing about a late-twentieth-century junkie, because, really, what character has been given *more* context than a Gen X dude who was cool, then dangerously cool, then dead? I'm in a stream polluted with VH1 *Behind the Music* specials about OD'd hair-metalers and televised interventions for strangers. The first twenty minutes are always the same—pictures of a *beautiful* child with *happy* eyes, scrolling under the voice of someone who absolutely cannot believe what happened next. Until every moment of their unaddicted life becomes a childhood memory, neon and unfocused.

Caleb's would be an amazing TV voice-over. Short, funny, imagistic, resisting critique. Caleb doesn't care about the vast space. He isn't curious about what was there. Why should he be? There is perfection in the simplified image if you trust it. Greatness, a precipice, nothing in between.

[NOTEBOOK, JUNE 16, 1996, "UNTITLED"]:
The dream and reality must coexist. And I must deliver. It's not about what's on paper or what I play. My reality must be (and virtually is . . .). By December, I'll either be pricing mansions on Long Island or I'll be in a rehab center, then working as a plebian. I must do now. And always.

Dave is in the uninvestigated space at the edge of Caleb's memory as Josh duct-tapes him to that desk chair. Dave is looking at his brother and thinking, *I should bash your fucking face in, you fat fucking bully.* He is looking at how small Caleb is and how big Josh is, and he is seeing torture. He understands. Dave, too, is small, and he, too, endures the whims of the monster. He actually thinks the word *monster*, because what else could you call Josh? People tell Dave he's dramatic, the kind of boy to hiss and writhe over a scraped knee, but he's not being dramatic about this.

Yes, technically, Dave is complicit in his cousin's torture. He cannot deny the feeling of his own hands on Caleb's flesh, cannot unhear the sound of skin yanked by tape. But there is a crucial distinction: Dave has no desire to be doing this. His nature isn't cruel. His nature is thoughtful, self-aware, the opposite of his older brother, who is so far from understanding the calibrations of how he makes others feel that he might as well be a goldfish swimming into the glass of its tank, over and over, learning nothing.

The people who only experience Josh for a few hours at a time, once every couple of weeks, can see him as precocious. But what seems precocious in manageable doses takes on a heavy awfulness when you go to sleep feeling it, wake up to it, are unable to live a life that isn't tainted by it. Dave is the chronicler of the moments that nobody else sees.

Caleb is in the chair now, strapped in, kicking his legs, and making a sound behind the gag that, amazingly, seems to be a laugh and not a scream. Dave watches his brother smile at what he's done. His smile is cold and blank. To call it sinister would be giving it too much credit. It's just teeth, big, white teeth with no connection to any human feeling, any shared experience. Dave watches his brother's back as he grabs the chair and wheels it down the hall. Dave lingers behind. He imagines the sound of the elevator door closing, then the sound of something snapping, then a crash. He lets himself feel relief.

Revenge fantasies carry through the years, and now Josh is

a teenager and Dave almost is, and nothing has changed except their father moved out so there's less protection. Josh has just slapped Dave across his face for no reason. Dave was standing with the fridge door open looking for leftovers. Then Josh entered the apartment, walked up to him, smiled his pointless smile, and swung.

He's strong. Dave reels and ends up on one knee. Josh leans down.

"Don't ever fucking look at me again," he says. "What makes you think you can look at me?"

Dave looks at the wall. Of course, something happened in the outside world that led to Dave getting hit. Something has always happened outside Dave's view that he must then take the brunt of. It has never not been this way. Dave has been attacked in every room of their apartment, at every time of day, alone and in front of company. He's been punched in the nose, kicked on the ground, choked until it was hard to trust that Josh would stop in time. And Dave has always known why.

Josh is bad at life. Josh is isolated. Josh walks around by himself for no reason, just loops of Roosevelt Island, going nowhere, building up directionless rage. Dave knows Josh has been in therapy for years, has watched the worried looks on his parents' faces after returning from a session. He's seen Josh wail, seen him swaddled by their mother in a way that no child over six should be, as she turned to Dave and said, "He can't help it." When Dave is feeling bold, too angry for restraint, he reminds his brother of these things—you have *problems*.

Beth heard the slap and now she's standing in the kitchen doorway.

She whispers Josh's name, as though preparing herself to eventually say it louder. She walks up. Dave sees the bones of her knuckles as she reaches up to rest her hand on Josh's shoulder.

"Stop," she says. It's a question, not a command.

Dave sees the back of Josh's head as he turns to face their mother. He stands up straight, puffs his chest out. Beth shrinks from him like he wants her to. She is backed against the stove, almost resting on the burners. Her raised hand drifts down to rest on her thigh.

"You're a stupid bitch," Josh says to his mother.

Dave begins to cry and he hates that. He closes his eyes and tells himself to stop crying.

"You bitch," Josh says. "You cunt. You can't tell me what to do, you cunt."

Then silence. Dave opens his eyes. Josh has leaned closer, teeth now only inches from the top of his mother's skull. He waits a beat, lets her helplessness sink in, and then walks to his bedroom.

Beth is a noiseless crier. She stands in the middle of her kitchen and shakes. From behind, if Dave didn't know her, he might think that she's laughing. The silence feels profane, and Beth won't look at Dave no matter how much he glares. She walks to the sink and begins to wash plates with a bright green sponge. Dave watches her hands move in tight, controlled circles until they disappear into suds. Her head dips into her chest.

When my father still lived here, he used to lie and say that one day Dave would feel a love for his brother so full and right that it would be impossible to question. *You'll grow up, time will pass, everything will soften,* he used to say. *You'll lean on each other.*

Dave doesn't believe that, because time has already passed. He walks down the hall, doesn't pick up his feet, lets his socks slide. He passes Josh's room and stops. The door is open a crack. He hears drumsticks beating on one cymbal with no real rhythm, until it sounds like a rainstorm. He takes a breath and shoves the door open. Josh stops beating the cymbal and says, *"What?"*

"You shouldn't be like that," Dave says. He'd hoped it would come out deeper.

Josh raises his eyebrows and says nothing.

"Why are you like that?" Dave says.

Josh stands and walks over to his brother. The floor creaks. Dave keeps his eyes on a poster of John Bonham, sticks blurred, tongue out. He expects to be hit again, but he isn't.

"You don't get to know," Josh says, which is such a stupid, self-important answer, and then he closes the door in Dave's face.

Down the hall, Beth has made it to her own bed. Her door is open, too. Dave watches her next. She's curled up, her face almost on her knees, taking up just one corner of space on the mattress, like she's trying to make herself even smaller than she already is. Dave still feels the heat from his brother's fingers on his face. He lifts his own fingers up and swears to himself that he can feel grooves on his skin where Josh hit him, grooves that will never fill or fade. He turns his cheek so that Beth might look up.

She stares past him. She's looking for Josh—even if it's just the sight of his white door closed, knowing that he is on the other side of it. Dave's face burns fresh. He looks at his mother, rumpled in the middle of this room that feels too big now. His blood is on her bureau from the time Josh chased him in here and shoved him in the back, sent him careering too fast to put his hands up. He spots a bit of it, reddish speckling that would be unnoticeable to anyone who isn't looking. Her eyes meet his, finally. They are brown and wet. They ask him not to say anything because there is nothing to say. They ask him to let her curl up and worry for her eldest. To let her watch his closed door until finally he opens it and that moment feels like a victory.

Josh's door stays closed, mostly, for years. When it opens, the air changes.

Dave is fifteen, walking to the kitchen, and he is summoned.

This has become the routine of their relationship—Josh stagnant, alone in there, Dave moving outside his door and then sometimes, without warning, getting invited in. They sit on Josh's bed. The posters have changed. Dave eyes the newest and most idiotic one, a Ferrari GTO, cherry-red, the ultimate trophy meant to be lusted after by boys in towns that he's never been to, dreaming of screeching along back roads and revving the engine for mall girls in parking lots. Josh doesn't have a license or a place to rev.

A bleached-blond fantasy is stretched prone across the hood of the car, her first-generation fake breasts mashed against metal. The poster's placement is pretty obvious, visible with a slight head turn to Josh lying in bed, so he can look at the tits and the metal and pound his dick into old gym socks that he leaves on the floor for Beth to wash. Dave has heard him at night. He falls asleep imagining his brother's face, manic, his hand a blur as he comes, looking at this two-dimensional portrayal of success.

In the mornings, Dave sometimes wakes to the sound of Josh doing push-ups under the poster, his exaggerated groans like he's pulling a semi-truck or is halfway through frantic porn sex. Some mornings the door swings open and Dave can stand silently, watch his brother's eyes fixed on the poster, face too earnest to be anything but funny. Josh pushes until his body is hard and swollen, set jaw jiggling with strain, and if he's not imagining a Whitesnake video, he's imagining himself in a *Rocky* training montage, and it's a toss-up for which of those things is lamer.

The more Josh tries to stand out, Dave thinks, the more he tries to make himself someone impossible to ignore, the more undefined, unoriginal, vague he actually becomes. Man has muscles. Man cuts sleeves off shirt to show muscles. Man wants car with woman on top. Man sees sunglasses on TV and man buys those sunglasses to look like TV man. Man has desire so man makes himself come. Rinse sock; repeat.

Josh has summoned him today, it seems, for an economics les-son in between sets. He points at the car on the poster.

"Guess how much," he commands. Dave doesn't know. "Guess."

Dave guesses wrong and Josh calls him an idiot.

"Okay, so can I go?" Dave says.

"Do you think Dad could buy that car?" Josh says.

"I don't know," Dave says. "Maybe?"

"Bullshit," Josh says, and Dave shrugs because this is the most pointless conversation being had anywhere in the world at this exact moment.

They sit in silence. Josh begins to poke his shoulder muscle and watch the skin form quickly back over his finger indent. This can be done alone. Josh is not kicking him out, which means that he feels the need for company, for some unburdening that is too much, too honest, for his small cadre of sycophantic friends.

"Why do you want to be so rich?" Dave asks him, surprised that he has spoken what he's thinking.

Josh stands up, just to loom.

"You're a fucking idiot," he says.

"*You're* a fucking idiot," Dave says, and the words thud with strain.

"No, you're the fucking idiot," Josh says. "You don't even know that when you're rich you can do anything. That's the point, you idiot."

Dave doesn't want an elaboration on *anything*. He wants to leave, find his friends, real friends, the kind of guys who manage to get laid without Ferrari posters or push-ups, and he wants to smoke a joint along the river. He wants to tell his friends about this conversation, and then pantomime his brother jerking off for them to laugh at.

Josh plants himself between Dave and the door. He smiles the smile that he always smiles, and the meaning, or meaninglessness, hasn't changed since they were little boys. He makes a list of all the things he's going to do when he gets money. He's going to leave. He's going to buy a ticket the day of his trip, first-class, not tell anybody, so they'll all have to know what it feels like to miss him. He's going to take cash out of a bank before he leaves and put it all in a suitcase. He's going to go on a sleaze tour of the world. He's going to fly into Thailand and start there, but that's too obvious for smut, so then he's going to head through Bangladesh, southern India, Sri Lanka. He's going to buy boats off the struggling fishermen who built them, motor to little islands where nobody goes who doesn't live there. He's going to fuck whores in every ramshackle village he finds. He's going to take girls who have never before been whores and make them whores, holding the money out as an answer to all their questions. He will have and they will have nothing, and so he will be infallible.

Josh laughs and looks for Dave to laugh, but Dave doesn't.

"Oh, Jesus Christ, lighten up," Josh says.

"I'm light," Dave says.

He watches his brother fill the doorway. He looks at his face and he doesn't understand. Josh's wants, the fury and extravagance of them, never feel right to Dave. They come without a clear origin. Josh already has things; Josh isn't told no. There is no excuse of having been deprived to make him want the way he does.

The setting changes, eventually. Josh moves out of their mother's apartment into a new one that their father pays for, waits behind a closed door for Dave to enter. The rest is pretty much the same.

Dave walks in with falafels after an NYU class. He expects to find his brother writing or fiddling on his keyboard, but instead Josh is standing in the middle of his living room, shoulders pulled back, smiling, holding his dick and pointing the head right at Dave like it's a TV remote. A condom, wrinkled and wet, banana-yellow, lies on the wood floor between them. Dave looks down and makes an involuntary noise appropriate for the situation.

"Don't touch it," Josh tells his brother, as though that's something Dave had been considering.

Josh urges him to come in, just step around it. Dave doesn't move. Josh launches into the story of everything that transpired to result in a used, banana-yellow condom lying on his floor. Josh tells him that they'd been standing right where he is now, him and the whore. He made her put her hands on the wood, bent her over fully, and then fucked her. He made her scream, not just because she was paid and had to.

Dave stares at his brother, which he does not want to do because that's what Josh wants, but how do you not stare at someone trying so hard for it?

Josh has a girlfriend. She's often here with him when Dave shows up, on the couch, quiet, no suspicion on her face. Dave lets himself be angry on her behalf now. That feels nice. She is a *good woman*, he reminds himself. He doesn't know her well, but she's always seemed gentle, at least, and it can be assumed that she's a good enough person to not deserve to sit oblivious on the same couch where her boyfriend rough-fucks prostitutes. Her name is Priya. She is South Asian of some kind—she never offers details and Dave never asks—and so every time he sees her it makes him think of Josh's proposed sleaze tour in his bedroom at their mother's place.

Dave likes to mull over the option of telling Priya about the sleaze tour, feeling righteous in the telling. Josh makes it so easy to feel righteous.

Percy, still a baby but already huge, slithers by Dave's leg, a cable rope along his ankle, and Dave jumps. Josh laughs and tells him to watch out for the monster. Dave tries to focus his thoughts on Priya, who is so beautiful, more beautiful now that she isn't here and he's staring at the full extent of how she's been wronged.

The first time Dave met her they sat in Josh's bedroom, Dave on the bed, Priya, posture of a childhood ballet dancer, rigid on a low chair. They were all going to go out to dinner, but Josh was in the bathroom, showering and primping, so they sat in his room to hear him as he talked through the door. Priya smiled every time Josh spoke. Dave was aware of being jealous of his brother. Josh, something in Josh, made this woman want him, made her happy when she heard his voice. Caleb was there, too, standing by the door, and Dave knew that he was also jealous of Josh, and that made Dave angry.

Priya was mid-sentence when Josh came out of the bathroom. She was facing Dave, and she didn't see him as he walked behind her, naked, still dripping. Josh held his finger to his lips and glared at Dave to stay quiet. Dave felt his own inability to disobey and he hated his silence. Josh dangled himself above his girlfriend. That was the best way to put it. He held the base of his dick and dangled it in front of her eyes, demanding her to look. She sighed and he held it a little lower, so it obscured her face.

Josh was waiting for laughter. Dave set his jaw and felt his teeth grind together. He didn't want to give his brother the satisfaction, but laughter was easier than silence. He giggled, regretted it. Caleb giggled, too. It was a timid sound, the noise a rabbit would make if rabbits could laugh. Priya said nothing, gave a wry smile, and resigned herself to sitting very still, as though this scenario had always seemed like a plausible inconvenience for her to wait out.

Josh got bored quickly. He kissed Priya on the cheek, gave a wink to Caleb and Dave. She didn't seem upset, and nobody spoke about what had just happened, so it felt almost instantly unreal. They went to get Chinese food. He put his arm around her, she rested her head on him, and it was possible to believe, walking down the street behind them, that nothing was wrong.

A few months later, the phone rings in Beth's apartment and Dave picks up. Josh is on the line.

"Get over here," he says. "Come now. Please."

Maybe it's because of the shock of hearing *please*, but Dave does not protest and he feels in sort of a haze as he leaves his mother, crosses the river, walks through Manhattan.

The door is open when he gets to the apartment. Josh grabs him, pulls him in, shuts the door behind him. His eyes are worried, which is nice to see. Dave wishes Josh would stop moving so he could look at those eyes and feel satisfied. Josh is saying, "Listen, you need to say that you've been here all night. You're my brother and we were just having movie night. That makes sense. We were watching a movie. What were we watching? What would we watch together?"

There is no answer for this.

"What did you do?" Dave asks him.

Only as he vocalizes the question does Dave realize the full expanse of what the answer could be. The line between Josh's wants and his possibilities has never felt so blurred. There is no one around anymore to check his impulses or to ask him why. How far does he go in this shiny new apartment when he is left alone?

Josh tells him the story and doesn't seem ashamed. He rushes through it without providing much detail, but what he says is enough, and Dave shapes a scene that is the ultimate confirmation of his suspicions. How could he not?

The prostitute was on her back on the leather couch. It was a humid night and her thighs stuck to the leather. She lay waiting, looking up. He came out of the bathroom and stood above her with the snake running along his shoulders. He extended his arms and Percy ran the length of his wingspan, the dark maroon pattern on the tip of his tail twisting as Josh grabbed hold and waved it. She followed his eyes.

Percy wants to play. Dave imagines Josh saying this line, Hannibal Lecter–ish, barely above a whisper.

She scrambled off the couch and started to back away. He walked at her like something out of a really bad movie. Percy writhed.

She snatched her tiny pile of clothes off the floor and ran out his door into the hallway. He didn't follow, just stood in the doorway, no longer smiling. She told him you can't just do that. She was going to fucking tell people about this, she said. He didn't respond. He stood, Percy heavy on him, and wondered who she could tell, what she would say, who would believe her. Maybe someone. Nothing had happened. He wasn't going to *do* it, but how might the story sound? She got in the elevator and he was alone. He felt alone.

Dave doesn't say anything. Josh doesn't want him to; he just wants his presence and an alibi. Dave listens to his brother talk himself down. Nothing happened. And who's she going to tell? And what's the big deal? Even if she's green, she's probably seen way worse. She's a whore; that's sort of the idea. And even if she does tell somebody, she's not a person you listen to. He's a handsome young man, freshly shaven, in a Manhattan apartment, with clean suits hanging in his closet.

"Fuck it, everything's fine," Josh says. He waves his hand, dismisses the issue. Dave feels himself nodding.

"You want to stay?" Josh says. "Stay if you want. I don't mind."

Years later, the phone rings again at Beth's place, and time is a gear that won't catch. Dave still lives with his mother, finally done with college but not yet ready to move, wary of being alone. And Josh is still alone in that apartment, a large part of why Dave is so wary.

"Come over," Josh says when Dave picks up.

Beth lingers at his shoulder, trying to hear something through the receiver. Dave shrugs her off.

"Come on," Josh says. "What are you doing? Nothing. You're doing nothing, you're scratching your balls. Come on, I've got to tell you something."

So Dave goes. He leaves his mother, crosses the river, walks through Manhattan.

They don't do much. They sit on the black leather couch. They watch cartoons from their youth, with bright placating images that they could always agree on loving. They laugh together. Dave remembers when Josh would call himself Captain America, call Dave a communist, leap on him, and start smacking his face in the name of freedom. He even brings that up and Josh laughs, agrees that it happened that way. They watch until it feels like silence needs to be filled.

A tampon commercial comes on, set at a carousel.

"So, little brother," Josh says. "Guess who's been shooting dope?"

He doesn't look at Dave. He stays sitting up with that forced weight lifter's posture, staring at the TV as though not in conversation with anyone.

There are emotional options available to Dave. Pure shock, though that would be a stretch. Sadness would certainly be appropriate. Perhaps a sudden geyser of brotherly compassion that Dave has never felt before, a revelation that no matter what he's done in the past, Josh is in *danger* now. But this is not a moment divorced from history. The first and only thing that Dave can think is that this is the final and greatest act of his brother's aggression. Percy slides across the top of the TV and nestles himself by the radiator. This is a dare, Dave thinks. Another taunting question. *What are you going to do, little boy? What do you make of me now? How can you possibly handle the life that I'm willing to live?*

"You should try it," Josh says when Dave gives him no response.

Of course that comes next. No confession here, just the challenge.

Dave lets his gaze wander, and everything becomes obvious now that he knows to look. The Bic lighter on the coffee table of a man who always chided smokers for their weak wills. The spoon lying on the counter of a kitchen otherwise immaculate. And, Jesus, the obvious one, the hypodermic needle lying next to the spoon, as though Josh spent hours staging the perfect still life of brand-new addiction. Is there blood on the needle? That would be a nice touch. Dave remembers waiting his turn in the doctor's office in Sheepshead Bay and hearing his brother's screams echoing. He was so terrified of needles that three gruff Russian nurses had to hold him down. Dave remembers Beth's voice, *Shh baby, shh baby,* until it was over.

Josh gets up, walks to the kitchen, and returns with the needle between two fingers. He points it at Dave like the tail of a snake.

"It's the greatest sensation you've ever felt," he says. "Just trust me one time. There's nothing else past this. This is where all feeling leads. You don't want to live a life without feeling, do you?"

"You want me to use that?" Dave says.

"Dave, I'm clean," Josh says. And then, "What, you don't believe me?"

They are both silent.

The only reason Dave doesn't walk out is the guilt. Josh knows it, too. Dave is the one who first got Josh high, and there's a feeling of responsibility in that fact that he doesn't want now.

Dave broke his arm in a pickup softball game, got overprescribed Vicodin, brought some to the apartment, and announced that life feels better when it is slowed down. And of course that's true. It really, really does. And he really did think that Josh would feel better, be better, when everything shimmered and lagged a little. And Josh *was* better. Their time together was less tense. Dave never loved his brother more than those first months when they shared an opioid daze.

Dave should have known what the end result would be. How could he have known? Still, he should have. Josh has to be bigger in everything. One perfectly good high—tidy pills, ready-made doses—isn't acceptable when someone somewhere is getting even higher. Dave eyes the tip of the needle, a new toy, so much cheaper than a bench press or a makeup kit or a girl from an ad in the *Village Voice*.

"What do you want from me?" Dave hears himself say, more soap opera than he intended.

Josh raises his eyebrows, lets that serve as an answer.

"Josh, this is fucking absurd," Dave says. "It's just . . . it's absurd."

Josh shrugs, then grins. He sits back down next to Dave and makes a show of how much better sitting feels to him now, like nobody has ever really *sat* before. He tilts his head back and lets his body sink deeper, his toes wiggling in his socks. He closes his eyes and relishes the last effects of a hit he must have taken before Dave arrived. Dave watches him let the feeling take over, oblivious to anything other than his own sensation, which is kind of what he's always cultivated.

Dave stands up fast. He remembers in a wave, every stoned scene that has brought them to this point crashing down, all the long and boring hours when Josh invited his little brother over so as not to be alone.

He remembers the first time Josh took Vicodin. Josh was nervous. Dave taunted him for that.

He remembers, months later, Josh no longer nervous, sitting on the couch and insisting that nothing tasted quite as good as cherry-flavored prescription cough syrup, which he bought when Dave didn't arrive fast enough with the pills. Josh wore a ridiculous silk smoking jacket, looked like Hugh Hefner on steroids. He took out a set of really nice tumblers, the kind that captains of industry pour aged whiskey in to celebrate a merger. He plucked three ice cubes from a bucket with unnecessary tongs, then cracked the childproof seal and gave it a sniff like he was a sommelier. He poured one full bottle into a single tumbler, perfect, right to the top, and began to sip. He sipped and talked about the future, mumbled vague screenplay ideas until he finished the syrup and finally looked pacified as he fell asleep.

Dave remembers the fake prescriptions they used to write, the pad that Josh stole from an old friend's divorced doctor dad. He remembers the closest they ever were in their lives, those frantic hours spent practicing signatures that were not their own, taking turns hitting different pharmacies so as not to be recognized.

What Dave doesn't remember is the exact moment when the trajectory of his usage veered off Josh's course. Moments like this are always imperceptible. Dave felt fear, the way you're supposed to, stopped hitting pharmacies, and slowed the habit. Josh sped everything up, packed his apartment with pills that were all quickly used or sold, rushed to replenish. Then there was that night when Josh came through the door, breathing hard, saying that a pharmacist recognized him even under the unseasonable winter coat and pulled-down cap, called him a fiend, and then called the cops as he sprinted out into the street.

"Jesus, how often are you doing this?" Dave asked.

Josh said, "Just shut the fuck up." And then, quickly, "Listen, do you have anything?" So much gentler than Dave had ever heard him.

Dave remembers all the nights when he couldn't force himself to leave. Josh would say stay, and so he did every time, watching and breathing until it was too late to stumble to the subway and return home.

Dave remembers willing himself to fall asleep on the couch, jeans still on, forcing his eyes to stay closed. Josh fell asleep first and Dave fell asleep frightened, the way it always had been and always was, like they were back in Sheepshead Bay as little boys, Josh lording on the top bunk.

And now it's needles. Josh pulls a bag out of his pocket, chunky powder the color of dirty snow. Dave doesn't want to stay to watch.

"Josh, I can't just sit with this," he says. "This is bullshit. What do you want me to do with this information? I can't forget it."

Josh waves his hand and calls his brother a drama queen. Dave gets mad, says, "Fuck you," and leaves. Josh doesn't say anything to stop him.

Dave walks to the pay phone on Lexington Avenue and roots around for a quarter. It smells like piss in the phone booth. Everything smells like piss all over this city, and Dave vows to leave and go somewhere green where nobody he knows has ever been. He finds a quarter. He holds the receiver to his ear, determined to share the burden of knowing what Josh is. He tries to think of who to call and what the person on the other end of the line might do, and there is nobody, there is nothing. He hangs up.

The last time Dave visits, the apartment stinks of sweat. The windows are closed and the air-conditioning unit is shut off. Dave looks over at it with longing.

Josh sees him looking.

He says, "No, no air."

He can't get warm.

"It's ninety degrees in here," Dave says, and Josh doesn't bother to disagree.

Josh lies along the couch, sweated black T-shirt molding to leather until couch and shirt are indistinguishable. How old is that couch? Dave can't think of Josh not on it anymore. Josh walking in the neighborhood, Josh standing in the kitchen making eggs—these are unbelievable images, fables. Dave's memory is already altered. It's like a Beckett play, he thinks, just a whole lot of scenes of two brothers in a barren wasteland with one couch, unexplained and never dragged offstage. Dave thinks of all the bodily fluids that Josh is potentially lying in—come and spilled blood, the runoff of satisfied vaginas if any of his stories are true, snake piss if snakes do, in fact, piss. Everything that he once celebrated rendered sticky and unwashable.

The image pairs well with the thrilling weakness of his brother's pose. Josh is lying down because he can't manage anything else. If Dave wanted to, if he was mean enough for it, he could stand above his brother and rain down on his face with fists, leave imprints of his knuckles on Josh's cheek, a long over-due payback for every day of their childhood. But he doesn't do that. Bullies leave you forever unsatisfied. You fear them and hate them and wait for retribution, and then the moment they lose their power they're too pitiful to treat the way they treated you.

Josh's belly button peaks out from under his shirt, and it looks like a sad mouth. Dave stares at the track marks on both of his brother's arms, bloody doodles, all the care to cover them in makeup, to pull his sleeves down, gone. He looks away and then is drawn back. He tries to find shapes in the pocks, order, finds nothing.

"I'm quitting," Josh says. "I've decided I'm done with it, so I'm stopping. It was fun, but now it's over. I just need company, you know. That's why you're here."

Of course. They watch TV together until it's dark out. Josh has rented *The Baby Sitters Club*. Dave calls him a creep for this and Josh says, "Shut up, it's calming, it's easy." They let the pretty faces and quick plots and bright green lawns wash over them in the dark. Dave is bored. He stops watching the action and instead watches Josh watching, his face lit only by the screen. There's his smile, twisted, impish, staring at teenage girls having a water fight on the Fourth of July. The face around his smile is new, bloated and slackened. His breasts quiver as he laughs at the dialogue.

What do you wish for, Brenda?

Best friends, forever.

Dave watches the flab shake. He would have teased him for that when they were boys.

"Don't look at me like that, fuckstick," Josh says. The voice, its pitch, its anger, is still the same.

"We should take you somewhere," Dave says.

What a pointless thing to say. Josh turns over enough to stare right at him. Dave refuses to blink.

"I'm fine," Josh says. "I've got it under control."

He dozes eventually, or at least he stops talking. Dave turns off the movie and the apartment is silent. This is the first time Dave has ever wanted to hear his brother make more noise. Jump on the pull-up bar, play the keyboard. Type something loudly, then print it. Speak. He says his brother's name and there's no response. He says it again. He leans his face close to Josh's mouth to make sure he's breathing. He is, and it sounds like a little boy blowing bubbles into chocolate milk. He smells like an old man, like vinegar and birdseed.

Dave stands to leave. He reaches out to touch his brother's shoulder, wonders why he's doing it as he does it. Josh doesn't move when Dave touches him, and Dave wonders if he'll remember that he was ever here.

Dave and I sit close, our knees nearly touching. I can smell bacon and eggs on his breath.

"I want to stop talking," he says.

"Okay," I say.

We're quiet together for what feels like a long time but isn't. We are never quiet together, never blank like this.

We're at my parents' place, and my father is in the kitchen pretending not to listen. As Dave's marriage has become increasingly irreparable, he's gone back to sleeping in my childhood bed, wearing my old flannel pajamas. My father has slipped into familiar routines of worry. Worry is muscle memory here. I feel it every time I visit.

When I was too young to know any better, my brothers were indistinguishable. They both dominated my consciousness. They both felt to me to be on the verge of something. They both understood that there were powerful, mysterious experiences to be had beyond that verge, and at night, in my mind, I would tiptoe forward trying to see. Then Josh sickened and died, and the precipice became simple and literal: It was the place from where he fell. Dave backed away, balanced, aged, but still they had been there together. I'm surprised at how jealous I am. I'm jealous now the way I was jealous then, though at this point I should probably know better. I want to feel what they must have been feeling in the early morning hours as they transgressed— a reckless, shared joy. Even when it wasn't joy, when it was hate, it was visceral—the emotion of potent lives mounting before the downfall, which was the boring part, the part that I got to see up close.

As a boy, I loved the Icarus myth for the subtext that the sensation of flight is maybe worth the fall. It's still the best kind of story there is, written from the aftermath with moralizing regret but full of all the sexy, shimmering details worth remembering, even if just as a warning. See: Milton, Augustine, De Quincey, Frey. Dave got the details, but he doesn't want them. He doesn't want to be a part of his brother's story at all, doesn't like the implications that story leaves behind, and so we're stuck on how to remember.

"Look," I say. "Please just tell me: Was any of this ever fun?"

I have chased my brothers' transgressions since I was old enough to transgress. The first time I smashed up a Vicodin and snorted it, it was, very consciously, an attempt at inclusion. I want to tell that to Dave now, lingering on every detail. I want him to see my girlfriend at the time, freshman year of college, her long, matted hair not yet in its eventual blond dreadlock form. I want him to see how her mouth hung agape, perma-stoned. And the homemade skirt covered in tube-painted Simon and Garfunkel lyrics that spun around when she hippie-danced.

She hurt herself skiing and was overprescribed. She came to my dorm room after my baseball practice, and we sat in the semi-dark on my bed as she chopped the pills with her student ID card and shuffled the powder around her ironic Hello Kitty makeup mirror. I thought of my brothers when I leaned my face over the mirror and saw myself, pale and fat, sprouting facial hair in awkward tufts on my neck, scars of white lines running across my reflected face. I imagined that Josh was there with me, not round and tufty, but beautiful, blinking back at me. And Dave was there, too. They were both watching. I imagined that we were finally peers, that I finally understood the value of sensation.

I was overreaching. I knew it even then. Because all I felt was tired and a little nauseous. And we would never be peers—one

brother was already ash and the other read education policy text-
books, ate stir-fry with his wife, talked to the cats, was in bed
by ten. And once the lull of the high started to fade, I returned
quickly to my truer nature, to the fear that Josh left me with. I
lay awake in bed and told my girlfriend that I worried for her.
I was sorry I encouraged her, and it was my responsibility to
help her stop. The impulse to do drugs and the impulse to perform half-assed exorcisms were and are equal in me. The result
is that lamest of party guests: the casual user who exaggerates
how good everything feels and then bugs the cool kids about
side effects.

Dave stands and says, "Listen, it wasn't fun. I'm going to the
kitchen, all right? I want food or something. I'm done."

I say, "Wait."

There's more that I want to tell him, a long list of ways that
I made up the connections I never experienced. My high school
band, how I sang Nirvana covers in the most earnest Cobain
impression I could muster. All the rock docs I watched and turned
off at the peak of excess, before the predictable final twenty minutes could unfold. The Burroughs books I read as conspicuously
as possible, picking crowded places outdoors on sunny days and
holding *Naked Lunch* or *Junky* up high. I performed these read-
ings. I pretended that I understood the sensibility. That all the
meticulous descriptions of bloody needle tips and wet assholes did
more than make me blush and laugh. I took the prologue of *Junky*
to heart and imagined it narrated in Josh's voice—the sneering
description of a quiet, privileged upbringing, what he referred to
as *the props of a safe, comfortable way of life,* all the while letting the
reader know that there was something else in him, unavoidable.

I want to tell Dave these stories. I want to make him see me
and how I've tried. I don't. I'm not sure why, but I hear myself
regurgitating an anecdote that I haven't thought about in years.

It's something safe and rehearsed, involving a bizarre family game of musical chairs on Rosh Hashanah. Josh cracked jokes about my dinosaur underwear; the whole family laughed.

"Do you remember?" I ask when I'm done. "It was funny, remember?"

Dave raises his eyebrows, then lowers them and gives a sad squint. He sighs. What do I want him to say? Why would he remember that? Why would anybody remember that? It probably never happened and even if it did it was an aberration born out of the kind of boredom that only Grandma's apartment could produce.

He shrugs and I snap at him. I say, "Come on, don't fucking shrug at me."

"I despised him," he snaps back, and suddenly he's in my face, neck strained, eyes awake.

"I despised him," he says again. "Not for what he became. I despised what he always was."

As Dave turns and begins to walk away, I imagine Josh on a black couch in a dark room, smiling a thin, threatening smile, his face in a way I never saw it. It's the kind of image that Dave has always walked away from, that he's always wished he didn't have to know. He's fleeing again, but then he stops in the doorway. He looks back at me. He returns to initiate a wooden hug, no arms wrapping, just stiff palms beating on backs. Still, a gift.

"Okay, you want to know a nice memory?" he says.

He says it slowly. He begins with, "This is stupid," but pushes himself into the description of a poem that Josh wrote at thirteen. It got published in the middle school yearbook, Dave tells me, so hundreds of families had it sitting in their homes. And then it was entered in some citywide contest. It didn't win, but it came close. Our father taped a copy on the fridge; Dave remembers that. It remains the most read thing Josh ever wrote.

"I thought he was so smart," Dave says. "Really, I did. He was."

He claps his palms together and rubs them like he can't get warm. He goes silent and I think he's finished, but then he recites the poem from memory. I'm surprised by how easily he recalls it, hardly any stumbling. He speaks it with care for the language, with beats where an author would have wanted them, the intended emotion whispering out from the end.

It's a really nice poem for a thirteen-year-old. For anyone, maybe. It's honest and it's sad. I want it to be a clue to something, but I don't know that it is. And, anyway, definite clues make for bad poetry.

[POEM, SPRING 1980, "LORD FEAR"]:
Behind an iron gate with a steel fence in an iron compound
There lives Lord Fear.
In his eyes is his cold, white stare.
His gun and his shield by his side, a metal sheet protecting his
    heart—
Lord Fear is frightened of what has never been.

Two months later, I'm at St. Vincent's hospital on Seventh Avenue because Dave tried to kill himself but then got too scared and managed to hail a cab before passing out. My parents are on vacation, trying to get a flight back home. They called and asked me to be present until they could be. Beth is on her way. I'm alone with him. No, that's not true. We're far from alone, but in the crush of the hallway of an overcrowded ER diagnostic ward, we only know each other.

He looks like a Hare Krishna, body robed, head shaved, eyes dulled, and I will myself not to think that. He is writhing. I have never seen a person writhe before, not really, but when I see what he's doing, I know that's what writhing is. He's strapped in, leather buckles pinching the skin on his wrists. A nurse tells me that, maybe half an hour ago, he had screamed that he wasn't the kind of person who deserved to be treated like this, had sprung off his wheeled cot and sprinted out onto the sidewalk. He was tackled by orderlies halfway down the block, hospital gown ripping, ass out in the wind. So that's why the straps.

"They fucking shaved my head to mark me as a crazy person," is the first thing Dave says to me.

I say, "Uh-huh."

We're in the middle of a wide hallway. He yells, *"Hello?"* at anyone in scrubs who passes. They don't stop moving, on their way to patients who need urgent care, and Dave curses at their backs as they go. I haven't seen this brother before. Not out in the open like this. I've slept next to him and woken to the sounds of his nightmares, but the moment Josh died, Dave's narrative became one of control and steady redemption. It had to. As I watch him, struggling against his straps, eyes feral, that has never been more clear.

A nurse stops, looks at my face, and says, "He's stable, hon. Just stay with him."

There are no seats available, so I stand above his cot and lean down. I surprise myself when I reach my hand out to touch his cheek. It feels like muscle memory, but it's a movement I've never made. I stroke the sweat off his stubble and I tell him he's safe.

He says, *This sucks,* over and over again, and when I keep rubbing his cheek and telling him it's okay, he switches to saying he's cold, it's so cold in here. There's a little blanket that he's kicked to the foot of the cot. I pick it up and try to cover him with it. It feels good to care for him, but then it hurts and my fingers keep losing grip on the blanket and I can barely keep his legs warm. I tell him that I don't want him to die. I think I actually say, "I'd be really upset if you died," which is ridiculous but feels deeply important to hear out loud. I used to think that if I'd said that to Josh, as bluntly and imploringly as possible, the force of my care would have been enough to combat what had become biological need.

"I don't want to die," Dave says. "I mean I did. I wanted to die so fucking bad, but then I got too scared. I was close. Do you know the feeling I'm talking about?"

The safe answer is no, so that's the one I give. The longer answer would be maybe, and certainly more so now. And also that it seems so easy to do the thing that will kill you because you don't like feeling how you feel. It never occurred to me how easy it must have been for Josh to die, how much easier, maybe, than all those years he worked to stay alive.

"I need you to do something for me," Dave says.

I say okay. He tells me there are pills in his backpack, lying on the floor next to us. Vicodin and Percocet and something else I can't recognize. And there's more at home in the little suitcase that he brought over to my parents' place. I make an involuntary surprised noise, and he says, "Come on," like this shouldn't be a shock.

"Flush them all," he tells me. "And don't take any for yourself."

I start to protest that last part to be funny, but he looks at me, so I say okay, again. I promise I'll come back and I leave. I start running down Seventh Avenue because that feels so cinematic, my willingness to wheeze just to make sure I destroy the danger in time. I stop after a block because I'm tired and this is stupid; it's not that kind of danger. I get a slice of pizza and I walk with it.

I shouldn't be thinking only of Josh. Not every danger is his. But memory conflates, especially if someone dies when you're still young enough to see only Woolf's bright caricatures, when you don't think much of anything but you feel everything. Josh's overdose is the most seismic event that has ever happened or will ever happen in either of his brothers' lives, an axis on which all other stories move. He *is* every thrill and every fear. There's no room for anything else, or there shouldn't be.

But soon I'm in my parents' bathroom, standing over the toilet with two bottles of painkillers. I'm hearing Dave and his pleas for my help, seeing his shaved white head, the scrapes on his arms. I'm the one concealing evidence this time, making sure that this incident can be isolated quickly in the narrative—just a little too much prescribed to ease the sciatica, just a bad day and an overreaction on the way back from the pharmacist. I think of Dave's memories of Josh on the leather couch where I sometimes slept, Josh making his brother hold on to the secrets.

It's not a premeditated thing, not a statement I intend to make, but there are my fingers reaching into the second bottle, pulling out two Percocets, high-dose. I pop them into my mouth and swallow hard and dry before pouring everything else into the bowl.

I sit in front of the TV for hours.

The phone rings and my father is on the line, far away. He asks how Dave is, and I say bald, which is the wrong answer, so I say okay, lucid, getting better. I watch a reality show about deep-sea fishermen and feel like my fingers are made of steel, mid-smelting. I hold them in front of my face and wiggle them to see them ripple, and then I laugh at myself because that feels like an amateurish thing to do. I walk back along Seventh Avenue and mumble my way through explanations at the hospital—who I'm looking for, what he's in for, which I can't really explain, where they've put him, which I don't know. They tell me where he is, but I get lost. I walk long loops around the hospital, peeking through open doors at tubes. I finally find him way up in the psych ward, the place for botched wrist-slits and failed ODs, sitting at dinner across from a very thin man, who starts to cry when I walk in. Dave is glaring at him, disgusted.

He sees me and doesn't say anything. I give a big smile-wave combination like this is visiting day at summer camp. I sit next to him and tell him my task is done. I think of Paul Newman eating eggs in *Cool Hand Luke* and fight the urge to laugh. He thanks me and says the food is horrible. He runs a plastic spork through mashed potatoes like he's raking a Zen garden. His ex-wife had a mini–Zen garden. I watched them rake it together, him looking up and saying, *I swear it really calms you, no bullshit.* We sit next to one another in a crowded room where nobody speaks. I ask if he wants his fruit cup; he says no, and I begin to eat.

I think that whenever somebody writes about an addict, the narrative is ready-made for them in stencil form if they want to take it—either the former addict writes memories of their past as though detached from it, with wry, wise regret, or a loving observer writes about their loved addict in isolation, as one person who fell into one hole, and if or when the hole closed around them it was tragic but there were no implications for anyone who knew them, just the tragedy. The bad-luck anomaly. That's the story we've been telling, all of us, from a sturdy, safe place we made up, from the quiet of lives that have settled around his absence.

But Josh is in the thick air of the messy moments of all the years that have passed without him. He is here with us, in this room where nobody wants to be, where anybody has the capacity to be. There is a face, his face, transposed onto all the faces that I look at and am frightened by, slurping fast dinners before waiting in line for the pay phone and hustling back to their cots. There are his eyes; I think I remember those clearly now, deep, layered brown and a little hidden. And there are his words, the ones that Dave spoke to me not long ago, words that feel like they underlie so much of what came next: *Lord Fear is frightened of what has never been.*

· · ·

Like me.

This is the first thing that Lena Milam thinks when she faces Josh. She is on Tommy Parker's bed in his mother's apartment on Roosevelt Island—on top of the sheets; they haven't yet been under together. Tommy is sitting next to her, close. He is narrow and gentle, gentler than any other fifteen-year-old boy Lena has ever encountered. He's holding her hand, and that makes her feel lucky. Lena is fourteen, and she, too, is narrow and gentle. Tommy is fit to her. She thinks of them like two parts of one machine that works.

Josh is the other part to Tommy. When they stand together, there is no similarity, just comedy, a mismatched buddy-cop vibe. Josh is tan and broad, and when he speaks it's meant for everyone to hear. Tommy is often at his elbow, pale and concave, a perfect straight man. Before Lena, they were always together. Now they are together less, so there's tension.

Josh walks into the bedroom and doesn't say anything. He looks at Lena and Tommy on the bed. Lena feels as though she's been caught, though she's not sure doing what. She pulls her hand away from Tommy's, and Josh laughs at that. She presses her fingers together like a steeple. She keeps her legs crossed at the ankles, and squeezes something invisible between her calf muscles. She rocks her torso just a little, the motion only noticeable to anyone who might be staring at her.

Josh is staring. He leans down, right in Lena's face. He

reaches forward, and the muscles on his forearms make little valleys where skin settles around strained sinew. His fingertips, calloused from drumstick wood, are pointed at her ribs, and she imagines that he might play her bones like he is a xylophonist and she is a pirate skeleton from a Saturday morning cartoon. Right before the moment when her body would have decided to flinch, Josh veers his hands away and grabs Tommy's arm, the intended goal from the beginning.

"Thomas," he says, fake-stern. "Thomas, it's time."

"No, man," Tommy says in a way that makes Lena think this protest has been planned. "No, hey, come on, man, it's embarrassing."

"Thomas, the lady paid for a show, and goddamnit, she's going to get one."

Josh winks at Lena. She feels queasy in a good way.

Josh has Tommy by the elbow and he yanks him up, escorts him into the space that has just been ordained a stage, the little square of blue carpet in between bed and door. Lena watches.

The show begins. It's mediocre, but spirited.

Josh is John Belushi. Tommy, theoretically, is Dan Aykroyd. They do *Blues Brothers* bits. They order four fried chickens and a Coke. They talk about Illinois Nazis. They call Lena a penguin. The accents are terrible. These are New York boys, and New York boys can only do New York accents.

Tommy stops after a while, his face adorably ashamed.

He says, "Okay, that's enough, I think she's seen the movie anyway."

She has.

"Get your ass back up here, my brother," Josh says, still in the bad accent.

He tugs on Tommy, somewhere between fun and threatening.

"Dance with me," he yells.

Tommy tries to make himself heavier, unmovable, but Josh kicks at his shins to get him stepping. It's funny. The effort is, at least, even if the impressions aren't. Lena begins to laugh, a surprised, gasping sound, holding her steepled fingers up over her lips. Josh seems nourished by this. He points at her, triumphant, and smiles. He has the most geometric smile that Lena has ever seen. Every feature is so large and defined that it has its own shape—rectangle teeth in a row, sharp diamond eyes, lips opening as wide as possible so that his mouth is stretched into a full trapezoid.

He begins to force Tommy to shake his tail feathers. He makes him dance like Ray Charles is playing an electric keyboard in the corner and they're surrounded by black extras. Josh dances, too, with abandon rarely seen in a straight male teenager. He dances up close to Lena, puts his face right in front of hers. She sees all the things he wants her to see, things hard to define—his force, his burgeoning beauty. Teeth, he wants her to see his teeth as he smiles. But she sees something else, too, equally hard to define. Maybe the best way to put it is *need*. For all the ways that Josh's body forms a physical command—*laugh, laugh now*—his eyes are begging. *Laugh, please. I need you to laugh.*

This is an important moment.

It is intoxicating to be fourteen and needed. Overwhelming, yet impossible to confirm. Lena scolds herself against Judy Blume self-importance, that joy of identifying as the kid who gets the *insides* of people when her peers see only a shell. But there is Josh dancing, and there are his insides shivering, she thinks, in need of someone's cupped hands and breath for warmth.

The show ends. Josh releases Tommy, shoves him, actually, back next to Lena on the bed. Tommy is breathing hard. He holds her hand again, palm now damp.

"How was that?" he says.

It's a loaded question, and Lena is still thinking of fear like a birthmark on Josh's face, so she just says, *"Great."*

She looks up at Josh, his chest heaving, unconvinced. There's a moment of panic, and then she laughs again. It starts forced, but it catches on inside her, and Lena laughs until her ribs hurt and she is hoarse, laughs until she snorts, clapping her hands like a zoo seal during a public feeding. Josh smiles.

"She's all right, man," he says to Tommy, like the only thing that has transpired in the past fifteen minutes is Lena looking to pass inspection. Lena swears to herself that she can see him slacken into momentary peace, as though he has finally exhaled.

Josh is waiting for her on the street before her first day of high school. She hasn't asked him to do this. She's hardly even seen him all summer. He looks like he feels as though he should be thanked.

"Thanks," Lena says. "You didn't have to do this."

Josh shakes his head with vigor. He says he will not entertain thank-yous, says it's nothing. She shrugs and they turn to walk together because that's the only thing to do. He doesn't put his arm around her, but it feels like he's been thinking about it. He hangs close, walks slowly so that he doesn't leave her behind. Their sides brush, her shoulder, his biceps.

Lena doesn't date Tommy anymore. She misses him and cries a lot. She feels hugely alone most of the time, alone like there is no matter around her. Then she feels ridiculous, goes to the bathroom sink and splashes cold water on her face until it's numb, which is also, she thinks, kind of ridiculous.

It seems like a long time since she has walked next to somebody. She decides that it's a nice feeling, and that Josh is nice for giving it to her. He's the only other person she knows who goes to the High School of Music and Art. She thought of him at her flute audition, and in her pre-September panics she has had only his presence to imagine, a school full of Joshes, their shoulders and laughter filling up the hallways.

He's wearing sunglasses, even though the sky is gray. He's wearing old Keds that squeak as he walks. He walks like a god-damned horse. Even as she feels him slowing for her, she is doubling her steps to keep up and make it casual.

"You're *slow,*" he says to her after a block. "No wonder you're always late."

"How do you know I'm always late?" she says.

"A guess."

"You know, it doesn't make sense to wear sunglasses on a cloudy day."

He stops and looks down at her with a grave face. "There's glare," he says. "Off the clouds. The sun is *stronger* on days like this. You're squinting right now. You don't even realize it, but I see you squinting."

He looks satisfied.

"You don't have to slow down for me," she says.

"Yes, I do."

They walk to the tram, the only way for a kid without a driver's license to get off the Island until the subway tunnel is finished. Ahead, Lena can see the metal pods creaking back and forth over the river on thick cables. The wind is angled straight at their faces, blowing Lena's hair into her eyes, ruining whatever her morning mirror time had intended to accomplish.

When they get on, the tram shakes in the wind. Lena is afraid, like always, of the fitful jolts of creaking metal. They can see all of New York City below them, and she imagines the feeling of falling into it, the sound of that crash. Josh looks down at her. He tells her that when he was a kid he used to be scared whenever he crossed a bridge. Not anymore, but he remembers the feeling.

On the uptown bus, it's like they stop at every corner, vibrating in idle, waiting for old women on their grocery runs. A man is standing over Lena's seat, rocking with each stop, zipper at eyeball level. Lena feels Josh next to her, ready to spring. Lena doesn't want to like that feeling, but this is a big bus full of strangers and she is small, and Josh is here with her.

They don't talk. He has his headphones on and she can hear music leaking out. She wants to lean in closer to see if she can recognize the songs. His drumsticks are in his hands, pattering on his jeans. She is pretty sure he's looking down at the top of her head. Their sides touch again. *This is mutual,* Lena tells herself. *We both need this.*

At the gates of the school, he doesn't say good-bye. He disappears into the mass of people who all seem to know him, and she is alone again.

"Comb your fucking hair," Josh tells her when she opens the door to her building. Lena isn't offended. It's always like this. A year of it now, their ritual repeated but never addressed. His waiting for her, her lateness, his running monologues about her hair needing a fucking combing, her clothes needing a fucking wash, her face needing, well, something, something to improve it. It makes him happy to admonish her, and it doesn't make her unhappy.

Lena steps out into hard drizzle, unprepared. She runs to Josh and he raises his coat up above the two of them. She nestles into the dryness. He smiles, embarrassed by his own chivalry. The coat is new, a black trench, too warm for the season, but it's a look that he has committed to and he does not commit to looks lightly. She tells him, "I like the look," and he says, "What are you even talking about?"

Lena slept through her alarm this morning and then woke in a panic, scrambling out of bed, stubbing her toe while scrounging for clean underwear. She said no to breakfast, pushing through the kitchen while her mother yelled something about nutrition and her sister sucked her teeth in judgment.

"You're not even late," Sister said.

"You sure you're not hungry?" Mother said.

"She just wants to be early for that boy. Can't keep *him* waiting."

Lena's sister doesn't understand. She assumes they're sleeping together because that's how she sees the world, as one big petri dish of people doing the deed and trying to keep it from her. But Lena and Josh aren't doing that, and even the thought is infuriating. They are just together in the mornings, on time. They shepherd each other through New York City at rush hour. It feels good. All fall it felt good, and in the winter, too, when they left mismatched footprints in the snow. And now in the spring, when he wears tank tops on sunny days, like the Roosevelt Island tram is Venice Beach.

Yesterday he wasn't there waiting for her and it ached. This is another thing she could never explain to her sister—how she paced waiting for him, then walked to his building, looked high up at a window that might be his, imagined him alone up there, watching her. How when she hurried out of the apartment this morning and saw him, she felt relief. He wasn't mad at her. He was okay. You can't explain a platonic longing like that. The steady weight of one promised hour each weekday.

"We have to stop," Lena says at the corner deli. "Breakfast."

She runs in and returns with a two-pack of Twinkies and a Coke. She holds them out, one in each hand, grinning, an offering—*Go ahead, Josh, tell me.*

"Jesus Christ, Lena," he begins on cue. "That is so fattening. There are five *hundred* calories there. And none of them are productive."

His lips are pursed. His head is angled down in disappointment. One clump of wet hair has curved over his forehead like a parenthesis. Lena almost slides it off with her finger, then doesn't. He looks right at her, posture rigid, only enhancing the superiority, dark and lucid irises like ink. He tries to snatch her food, but she's expecting this and pulls away too fast, hides her daily corn-syrup doses behind her back.

She sticks her tongue out at him. He marvels aloud at his own patience, says that when he stands over the premature grave where Lena's total lack of willpower will take her, he will not feel responsible or even sorry, not even a little.

"Bury me with my Twinkies," she yells, and he laughs and that feels good.

A pigeon dive-bombs them, streaking toward Lena's unkempt hair. She flails at it with her Twinkies, her can. Josh shrieks in spite of himself, a noise so preposterous coming from him. Their eyes meet and now they're both laughing, until the laughing runs out and they're just breathing.

In the pause, Lena wants to ask why he wasn't waiting for her yesterday, why he does that sometimes, and does he know what it feels like to stand and wait, how small she is on wide sidewalks, the way doormen look at her with pity? She wants to grab him by the elbow and say, Jesus, of course she knows it's hard for him some days. She sees the frail parts of him, and if anybody can understand when he doesn't want to go outside and see all the faces moving past, closing in, it's her. She notices on the mornings when he comes down with drawn eyes, without having bothered to wash his face or brush his teeth, when mushed cereal and chewed fingernails are sticking to his gums. It's a small thing, but she notices. He can try to explain if he wants to. She'll listen.

Josh reenters his monologue, undeterred. "If there's any time you shouldn't be eating junk, it's the fucking morning. It sets a bad precedent. Your day is ruined. Right now, you are actively ruining your day."

She nods. He continues.

"Your hair's all dirty, you could fit five people in that shirt, you're drinking a Coke at eight in the morning. And then the Twinkie. Like a fucking hobo."

Does he realize that she baits these moments for him?

"Seriously, tell me what you'd think of yourself if you saw you on the street."

He speaks loud enough for any stranger around to hear, and fellow commuters grin at the back-and-forth as they shuffle to the tram. Young people caring, what a thing to look at. She feels the rain angling in, wetting the bottom of her jeans. She sees him notice this, mid-rant, and pull closer, wrapping them tighter under his trench coat, dry.

At the bus stop, she paints his face. She moves slowly, as tender as she can, trying to get his every detail right. It smells like piss in the bus stop, but Lena breathes through her mouth and concentrates. They're never closer than this. He has relinquished control. His eyes are closed for her. She watches their involuntary flutters as she rakes mascara along his lashes, and thinks of how thin a layer it is that keeps our eyeballs from anything that might hurt them. His lashes are long and cresting. *You could be a pretty girl,* she thinks, though she would never tell him.

He is ashamed of his acne, which really isn't that bad. He is ashamed, too, Lena thinks, of his need to cover it up, his inability to tolerate flaws that are so common. It would be impossible for him to allow the general public to see a pimple. But he's no good at the makeup and so he trusts Lena, only Lena, to do this. She feels her hands tremble still, always, as she decorates him, hiding the ritual as best she can with her narrow body.

With practiced, careful hands, she runs concealer in generous swaths across his face. She paints his eyelids, tries to contrast that blackness with a nice, subtle rouge on his cheeks.

"Almost done," she says.

He opens his eyes, and right away they're moving in darts, finding strangers that might be looking at him in judgment.

"Nobody's looking," she tells him. "Hold still."

She finishes and he turns away from her.

He doesn't say thank you. He never does. He reaches for his hair, sculpting it with the rainwater, making it match his clothes, his body, his face. When he turns back, Lena gives him a thumbs-up and he snorts, and she wonders if there is any lamer gesture in the pantheon of human gestures than a thumbs-up.

On the bus, dancer girls look at Josh, and middle-aged women, and businessmen, too, feigning casual scorn when Lena knows that they feel envy, maybe lust. He is happy, undeniably, for these moments. She likes thinking that she has helped make him happy. He relaxes a little into his seat. He takes his headphones off and surprises her by placing them gently over her ears. He leans in and says, "I love this song more than anything. Listen."

She thinks it's the most haunting song she's ever heard. It's Roxy Music's "More Than This." It's slow and mournful, and they're both high school art students who believe that all mournful things are genius, have consequence. More than this, the singer tells her, you know there's nothing more than this. And it doesn't feel overblown to think, Hey, yeah, he's right.

"I love it," she tells Josh.

He grins and takes his headphones back.

When they get to school, he messes her already messed hair with his fingers and walks through the front door ahead of her, doesn't turn around. She finds her people, underclass wind instrumentalists—shy trombonists, overcompensating piccolo masters. She stands with them, clumped against a remote section of lockers. Josh, armored in her makeup job, strides through the hallways, greeting, getting greeted. He stops at no group, offers nothing more to anyone than a quick grin, a few words or maybe a two-fingered salute. Lena watches him greet Youngblood Haskell, the prettiest and broodingest of the school's pretty, brooding skinhead painters. The hallway seems to part for them as Josh leans into Youngblood, says something funny enough to make this boy with so much invested in his own seriousness laugh.

Lena wants very badly to someday speak to Youngblood Haskell and is very certain that she never will. Josh won't introduce them. She won't exist, not in any visible way. But she's included by association, and she's proud as she watches Josh, swaggering and fragile, earning laughter. How terrifying it must feel for him in the second before he gets a response, how blissful when the laughter comes.

Lena will never tell anybody about those mornings when his teeth are unbrushed, his eyes red and darting. She won't tell about the flecks of Cheerios stuck on his gums, the smell coming off him when he's been thrashing in a panicked lather all night and hasn't bothered to wash. She won't tell how she breathes through her mouth to tolerate closeness, refusing to slide farther away in her seat because of how awful it would feel to shame him like that when he is already so shamed. How they can be silent together on the walk, then the tram, then the bus, and she won't push him to talk because to open his mouth might reveal something grotesquely weak, something that he can't take back. Those moments are hers.

Homeroom bell rings. He is gone. She will see him tomorrow.

———

It's over too quickly. The last journeys of Josh's high school tenure are tied to that feeling, an internal countdown for Lena. How many times have they done the same thing, developing toward nothing but an end?

"At least three hundred times," she tells him on the bus. "We've gone to school together exactly the same way at least three hundred times. And now it's just going to stop."

This is a sad thing. She wants him to confirm it. He won't. He starts poking her cushionless ribs. *Look, look, look.* She slaps his hand away. C'mon, he says. He puts his arm in her face and flexes.

He wants her to touch his biceps. He's been doing something different with his weight routine. More reps or more weight, one or the other. It doesn't make complete sense to her, but it means that he's no longer defining muscle and is instead adding bulk. For college women. Because older women like bulk. He flexes harder, reddening from all the flexing. *Touch it.* People are watching. *Touch it.* She relents. She pokes his biceps. It doesn't move. It's like overcooked steak, she thinks.

"Feel that?"

"What am I supposed to be feeling?"

"Come on."

She sighs and says—God, she can't even believe it as she says it—"It's big," and he gives a full trapezoid smile, head swiveling around the bus looking for eye contact, confirming for all commuters that, yes, she touched it and, yes, it's big. He throws his fists up over his head, simulates a crowd roar in the back of his throat.

They won't see each other again once there isn't a scheduled reason to. She knows that, and she is even a little proud of her lack of delusion. There won't be a place for this anymore. Oddly, Lena feels less like she's being abandoned and more like she is abandoning him. Who will armor him for a day of other people's eyes when he's in a freshman lecture or a crowded dorm room and she isn't there to help? How can she let him do his own costuming?

Lena, touch it again. Come on, Lena. Lena, do it, come on.

This time she tries two fingers, jabs her middle and index hard into his biceps, determined to make skin dent. She feels her face scrunching up with the effort. She is not this girl by nature. She will never be this girl again. She wants to ask him what they'll do when he's on college break. She has vague ideas of taking the tram over the river on Christmas Eve, lights on the water below them, Empire State Building in front of them, red and green. But that's not the kind of thing they do.

She wants to ask if he'll be okay, but she wouldn't be able to get more specific.

"We'll still see each other," she says instead, stuck between an assertion and a question. He says nothing in response. He cares. She knows he does, even if he doesn't want her to. Care is in every movement he makes, in the way his eyes glance at her, then away, then back again. Still, she'd have loved it if he said something.

She hears his voice once more after high school, through a phone. It's six, maybe seven years since the bus and the makeup and the muscles. Lena is out of college, working her first real job, occupying one half of a cubicle, an assistant at a publishing company on Madison Avenue. She's just a mile or so from the auditorium where they both had their graduations, Josh first, Lena watching in the back with her flutist friends. That was the last time she saw him. She has thought of him, yes. She tried to explain him once to her college roommate, stoned—*We never even kissed.*

Her desk phone rings and she jumps. It's still a surprise when a stranger in another office somewhere is directed intentionally to her. She lets it ring three times and then picks up.

"Hi, this is Josh from Pinnacle Paper," says the person on the other end of the line.

His voice is the same. She doesn't need a last name to be sure. She can't speak, and she hears her breath, loud, crackling through the line.

"Hello?" A sigh.

There is no indication that he's called for her specifically, no excitement in his voice. This is a price-per-volume call, a pitch. His job is worse than hers, lower, more mundane. She realizes that. It stings. She imagines him at a desk in a warehouse, cold-calling from a fat binder, trying to convince bored publishing underlings to tell their bosses to turn his blank reams into units of someone else's art.

She feels her palm sticking to plastic.

"Oh, oh hi, it's me," she says, finally. "It's Lena."

"Oh," he says.

She'd heard from Roosevelt Island friends that he had a band, that they'd gotten a few gigs. This made sense and she was happy for him. Then she heard it was over. She'd heard he was starting to write songs, had his own production company. It was vague, but she liked the idea of him bellowing orders, imagined him with a movie director's megaphone. She hadn't heard anything else.

She forces herself to speak before he hangs up, her voice too big and eager, trying to fill awkward emptiness with over-whelming cheer.

"How *are* you? Oh my God, small world! Paper, huh?"

His embarrassment leaks through the phone. She can picture something shivering in his eyes, his face fifteen again in her mind, and nobody next to him at his desk to help him by staying close. She wants to stop and start the conversation over, remove the crazed squeal from her voice. There has to be an unpatron-izing way to say, *I care for you. You are better than where you are now. I believe that.*

He starts talking about paper prices. He says that he can offer her boss a better deal than anything he's currently got. He promises that.

Lena looks down at herself—the khakis, the white blouse with a cluster of unnecessary buttons up around her neck. Payless work shoes, sensible chic. Yes, she feels ridiculous, and no, she's not exactly happy. But still, fine, it's to be expected. This is a quiet beginning to a settled life that is, and has always been, appropriate for her. It doesn't bother her that much to think about it. He's the one who isn't meant to be in this conversation, but he keeps going, flat and almost mean with his persistence.

Lena stays silent through Josh's pitch, and when he's done she offers no counter. It would have been good, hardball negotiating if it were intentional.

"Well then, look, if there's no wiggle room, I've got to go," he says.

She wants time to think of something to say.

"If you're happy with your supplier, that's fine," he says. "Keep us in mind."

She hears the phone click on his end, and she is returned to her high school self, the sound of a hang-up enough to make her limbs heavy. She holds the receiver to her ear until she hears a dial tone. She thinks of him on the bus. She thinks of the two of them, surrounded and alone. She tells herself that she will see him again. It's just a matter of waiting until he wants to be seen. Seeing him on his terms. The two of them on the bus in the morning, older, happier, too, but him still flexing, her still poking his arm to make him smile.

"You look like him," Lena tells me. "The way your hair falls on your face a little."

We're sitting across from each other at a scratched wooden table. Her irises move in small, concentrated circles as she takes in my face. I imagine that, in her mind, a vintage city bus sprouts around us, closing us in, a seamless set change to the New York of her high school memories. But we're in Park Slope, and nothing moves backward in this sleepy paradise of cafés and real estate offices and swarms of children who can correctly identify cilantro at the market when their parents want to show off.

Lena's twin daughters are probably out of their bath by now, their father wrapping them in yellow towels and drying their hair. She keeps apologizing that she will have to leave for home sooner than she wants to because she doesn't like the girls falling asleep before she lies next to them for a few minutes, so that they can feel her. She likes to stay for that moment when their faces change as they begin to dream.

Our hands almost touch as Lena reaches out her wallet to show me photos of the girls, sitting with their heads cocked in opposite directions, wearing matching checkered dresses, little tablecloths with eyes. She snatches her fingers back, thin, elegant fingers, flutist fingers. I picture their narrow tips on Josh's arm in the same spot that my own fingers would touch a few years later but with less grace. I imagine her teenage head like my child's head, tilting up at him.

The bar we're in is beginning to fill with thirtysomethings. Faded sleeve tattoos snake down bare arms, stop above sensible leather-band watches and wedding rings. Scarves are stuck into the armholes of peacoats before they're hung on iron hooks. First dates begin with quick hellos and mangled cheek-kisses. "Tainted Love" begins to play, not the original, soulful version, but the cover that epitomizes every stereotype I have of a bouncy, metallic eighties adolescence. Faces lift. Lena smiles down at her hands. I watch her fingers tap on the table.

"Hey, that Roxy Music song I was talking about, do you know it?" she says.

"Yeah, of course," I say.

She straightens up and smiles. "He must have played it for you. When you were a kid? Did he? He loved that song."

"Oh. No. It was in that Bill Murray movie a few years ago. What's it called? He sings it drunk at karaoke. The soundtrack was really popular when I graduated from high school."

She sags and I wish that I'd lied. Josh is so deeply past tense that a song he loved new has reseeped into popular culture as something for a faded star to sing as he attempts to reignite. I watch her realize that. As a sort of penance, I tell her the story about me on Josh's lap in the home movie, when he pieced together "Let It Be" on the piano.

"Oh, that's lovely," she says. "What a nice thing to remember."

"He taught himself to play the piano," I say.

"I know," she says. "Isn't that amazing? To have an ear like that?"

She thought of him today, she tells me. She dropped her girls off at school and she waited for the bus home alone. It was cold rain all morning and she'd forgotten an umbrella. She felt her hair, stringy, nearly frozen, sticking to her face and her neck. And then he was next to her, telling her she'd never looked worse, like seriously never ever, until she laughed, and then he put his headphones over her ears and watched her listen to his song. When she thinks of him, there is always music and she is always laughing.

"I was thinking about him for a while," she says, "and then something went off in my head like, hey, he overdosed. That's so strange. Sad, too, but more just weird. He had so much will-power. He was so healthy. When I was a teenager, all anybody around me felt was apathy, and he had so much conviction. If anybody didn't need drugs to feel things, it was him. You know what I mean? He was so *much* on his own."

She acts out *much*. She balls her flutist hands into narrow fists, presses them on the table. I nod my head at her, eager, agreeing with the feeling of the word as she uses it, a feeling that I know I remember. It's not just sad that the gentle Adonis she knew became a junkie; it's a surprise narrative. A fluke. It doesn't make any fucking sense. And the senselessness is kind of absolving.

Those people who shit themselves when they nod off on the subway, they are not him. The scabby punks who live on benches in Tompkins Square Park with arms that have turned to leather, who told me dope stories in exchange for pizza, they are nothing like him. That is what we're agreeing upon. I feel momentarily certain. But then. But then those scabby punks went to high school once. Even if they dropped out, there was at least a year when they sat on the bus and somebody probably sat next to them who found something *much* in them, indulged in fantasies of their lives that involved a different future. Everyone at this bar knew someone like that. And as the microbrews flow, if I went around and prodded each stranger, they'd find slurry details to remember, muscles and drumsticks, geometrical smiles with ominous unbrushed teeth.

It's the commonness that's most wrenching. Lena fights the commonness with care. Lena takes the common moments and breathes into them until they inflate.

"He deserved so much better," she says, spreads her palms on the table, flat and certain. "If there was anyone who deserved . . ."

She coughs needlessly. There is toast slathered in locally sourced goat cheese between us, meant to be shared, which she hasn't touched.

"Finish it," she tells me. I do and she watches.

"You really have his hair," she says. "Did I tell you that already?"

And then, "I don't want you to think that I'm weird for caring this much. Do you think that? I mean, it was just a few years that I really knew him, right? We never even kissed or anything."

I say, "No, it's nice." I surprise myself with how fully I mean it.

"I think some people, you care for them more because they need more care," she says. "That's not a bad thing, needing care. Or caring."

When we leave the bar, we walk side by side down a very different part of Flatbush Avenue from the one I live off. I keep my hands in my jacket pockets and say, "Brrr," and she gives me a little smile. She tells me that her girls like to say *brr* like that. They like the way it makes their lips feel. Sometimes Lena and her husband and the girls stand in a circle and *brr* at each other. She says it's silly but it's just one of their things. I realize how much I don't want to know about their things. Josh fades against their things. Their things don't seem silly at all.

"I think of Josh more now than I did for a long time," she says. "It's because I'm a mother. I look at my girls and I think about him. When they make me laugh. I laugh and I look at them and they're so beautiful but they're so breakable. Sometimes I leave the room and then I rush back to look at them again just to make sure."

She stops, embarrassed, eyes down, lips pressed. She shrugs. The wind picks up, and she snatches for her hat to make sure it doesn't fly off. The skin of our cheeks is pressed back, and our eyes squint at each other, our backs rounded. I put my hand out behind her because it looks like she might fall.

"That was a sweet thing to do," she says when the gusts calm.

I think I see a rat weaving across the sidewalk, losing itself in the sewer. I think I see another one, or maybe it's two, burrowing in the slush in a tree pit.

"If anything makes sense about the overdose, it's that he was alone," she says. "Underneath it all, he was too tender to be left like that. I think about how that must have felt for him. Nobody touching him or hearing him or anything. Doing, well, what he was doing. I hold my girls tighter."

In the years after Josh's death, I spent a lot of time trying to read my way to knowing what his high felt like. It started with Nirvana lyrics, but those never made sense. Burroughs came next, and Ginsberg, naturally. Now I look further back to Thomas De Quincey. I found this passage near the beginning of *Confessions of an English Opium-Eater*, and when I first read it I didn't like it:

Eloquent opium! that with thy potent rhetoric stealest away the purposes of wrath; and to the guilty man for one night givest back the hopes of his youth, and hands washed pure from blood; and to the proud man a brief oblivion for wrongs undress'd and insults unavenged.

I didn't like the idea of the drug having its own rhetoric. Because I had scattered memories of my brother on the nod, the way he would forget his sentences halfway through, robbing him of language that once came so easily. And I didn't like the idea of the drug giving anything back, when all we ever talked about was what it had taken from him.

But the passage is in my head now, clear, as Lena describes her breakable little girls, the way they need her assurances to fall asleep. What did Josh want more than whispers that he was okay, no, far better than that? What did he need more than a companion, hands on his face at the bus stop, covering his blemishes? He was already alone, Lena knows. Alone when he looked like a bodybuilder, alone in a rush-hour crowd. Maybe heroin was one kind whisper in an empty room. There is no *much*ness in that revelation, nothing sexy, just a quiet and obvious truth: People deserve to be held by something.

We get to the subway entrance, and there's no longer a reason for us to be together. There is rumbling beneath our feet. I'm missing my train.

"I have to go," Lena says.

She leans her torso in for a hug. She squeezes once and says, "I'm sorry if I sounded stupid. I remember watching him at band practice in high school and him looking really, perfectly happy when he played the song right."

[NOTEBOOK, JANUARY 23RD, 1991, "NOTES"]:

What really freaks me out is how I "fall from grace" every day. Because the mornings are usually symptom free. Most of the time, it's lurking in the background. Then the day progresses and I'm totally in it by night. And it's chronic then. One thing I can do is tell myself not to expect too much all at once. So when I feel good in the morning, that's when I tell myself that I might (probably will) feel worse by the night. This way, at least I won't feel frustrated or like I failed (just bad—really bad).

This is some of the earliest writing of Josh's that I have, not quite his high school self, but still, missives from his unaddicted early twenties. I read looking for something as close to innocence, as far from subterfuge, as possible.

He wrote these words on an early page of a notebook that he decided would contain the story of his emotional life. The rest of the page is dedicated to a super-pouty Morrissey quote, a motif that continues until he begins writing *See: Morrissey the God* and then simply *M.T.G.* at the end of many of his paragraphs. Another motif is *D.P.* It pops up constantly, even on the front cover, written in dark green marker, triple underlined.

He used abbreviations whenever he referred overtly to his *depersonalization*—the best word a therapist had ever given him for overwhelming anxiety that he couldn't shake, those moments when he lost control and viewed his own existence through stained glass, frozen, unable to breathe. After a childhood in and out of therapy, starting before there was really a language to put to what he was feeling, he clung to the right term when it was finally given to him. But he didn't talk about it; I never heard the word out loud. Now, I flip through his pages, and I see *D.P.* hounding him, and I think of Lena next to him on the bus on those days when he couldn't bring himself to speak.

He wrote these words right around the time he had his last accidental conversation with her, and I look for a description of that specific shame. He so rarely wrote in specifics, rarely wrote even in scene. Her name appears nowhere. Still, I'm surprised how quickly I find her perspective bleeding through every page, through each admission and plea. She saw him; his words confirm it. He wrote the sentiments that she always wanted him to express to her—how *hard* a day could be, how much he needed support. How he didn't want to feel like a failure as he tried to fall asleep, and how easy it is to fail.

These are, I think, words reaching out for a voice to call back, and I imagine Lena on the other end of the line willing him not to hang up until she's found the right thing to say. She saw him, underneath the beauty that she helped cultivate. She saw him soft and afraid and trying, but that self is soon pushed from his writing, consciously sublimated, as opiates begin to whisper, then to yell, to tell him that he is the opposite of afraid. I still read fear in the subtext, hiding, but the persona changes. A new language takes over.

[LOOSE-LEAF, JUNE 13TH, 1995, "THOUGHTS"]:
I am in my cocoon now. But when I burst forth, I will be a cobra instead of a butterfly. Never married! Fucking! Fuck women, as a race. Fuck them as I did and I do, as vengeance for my teenage years. You pathetic creatures will have to suffer your fate. I will be rich, a public figure, diesel, but these times will remind me never to sell my soul to creatures. Love? Love is hate. What most people refer to as love is for glorious pursuits and ultimate rewards.

Love is the juice and the candy. Long live power and its glorious unattainable end! Long live intoxicants! Long live vengeance! Long live misogyny!

I want his soft younger writing and the self that came along with it to feel original as I mourn its loss. It isn't original; I know that. He writes about flirtations gone wrong, about feeling like, *What comes next in the grand tragedy of my life?* He uses words like *azure* when he wants to be poetic. He quotes liberally from lyrics that, without a melody to elevate them, are just terrible. Even the torture of depersonalization can sometimes seem flat on the page; it was hard to express how awful that felt without reaching for language that rendered it common. Still, there is a churning underneath the pleading poetry, and that churning feels real, realer definitely than the soapbox preacher of self-reliance that took over so often after Lena knew him, the one that said he hated women and love, hated anything but strength and sensation. I can hear Lena's voice now when I read his stoned rage— *I see you in there.*

She will think of him tonight as she holds her little girls until they fall asleep.

. . .

Way out at the end of Brooklyn, Josh is five years old, in his mother's arms, trying to explain.

He is trying to tell her what these moments are when she feels like she loses him, when he loses himself. He settles on a word. He calls them *glimpses,* as Beth holds him by the shoulders and crouches to his level. She can see what the word means. It's in his eyes, fear like an iron gate swinging shut, until he's howling syllables but no words, punching the air. He sees shadows moving toward him, ceilings collapsing. He feels his body like hissing steam. He is outside that body, only able to peer in, not help himself. Beth has to hold him in the kind of wrap-up that lifeguards are taught to use on the drowning.

He looks like he's drowning. But then, competing with that image, there's the word, *glimpses,* and the fact that her five-year-old has the capacity to attach vivid, metaphorical language to his feelings. In the middle of this storm in him, he can stop and articulate. Beth debates telling him that's a lovely word choice he's made, but then a small flailing hand catches her ear and all she says is, "Ow, honey, stop please."

Beth has spent a good portion of her life coaxing boys out of nightmares. She was a leaned-on older sister, then became a mother not long after moving out of her childhood home. She's always been good at swaddling. But it was easy with her brothers. They woke up from what was so awful.

None of that was real, she could tell them, without lying. *You were sleeping, and sleeping doesn't count. Monsters are for sleeping. This is what's real. Brooklyn is real. I'm real.*

What do you say to a child about a waking nightmare? Josh's eyes are open; it's reality that frightens.

It's noon and already she's been embarrassed today. The phone rang while she was doing dishes, and the moment she heard that drawn-out nasal hello from Miss Greenberg, kindergarten czar, Beth knew what was wrong.

"What's wrong?" she said anyway, and Greenberg, voice humid with disdain, said, "Oh, dear, you should probably come take a look for yourself."

In the classroom, Greenberg trapped Beth and her problem child in the corner by the cubbyholes. Josh vibrated in Beth's grip. All the other children stared with round eyes, every one of them as angelic as a grape-juice commercial. They seemed to already know to be silent and somber, not to tease, when Josh got like this. They were concerned, and that made the contrast even starker. Josh had been going to therapy for a few months, and Beth hadn't been able to bring herself to tell any of the other mothers. It felt like that would be extra confirmation for the reports that she was sure these kids were giving as soon as they got home from school—*that poor boy was at it again.*

"Honey, stop," she told him, as quietly as possible.

And then, "Please stop."

And then, the words ripping from her, *"Tell me what I can do for you."*

He howled down the hall of the school, and into the car, and all the way home along Ocean Avenue. He howled in the parking lot, in the lobby, in the elevator, his cries echoing off the metal until Beth felt the sound pulsing behind her eyes.

The moment the apartment door opened he ran away from her. She found him in his bedroom, just a lump under his covers, finally quieting. He pushed his sheet until it slid off him, and there was his face, eyes scrunched tight. He stood up to run again, and that's when she got him by the shoulders, crouched to his level, asked him to explain, please explain.

Now she sits outside his room and waits for him to get hungry and emerge. After finding the right word, after giving her *glimpses,* he shut off. He's offered her no more explanation or affection, or even acknowledgment. She hears him breathing in there. She thinks of all the things she's done wrong: She crashed the car once on the West Side Highway when she was pregnant and has always worried that she broke him inside her. She ignored him when he cried as a colicky baby, let him exhaust himself because she once read something about self-soothing.

"I'm sorry," she calls into the bedroom.

He says nothing back.

"It's my fault," she says. "Whatever you're feeling is my fault. I'm sorry."

Still, he says nothing. She can't see him and she can barely hear him, but he looms. He expands; he fills the hallway. He is all around her. How can she not think about her son, who she made this way?

He never stops looming.

On the deck, in the backyard of a house in Rockland County—cedar-shingled, two-car garage, hedges bought full-grown—he looms. My father's business partner lives here, and when the family visits, the countryness of the place is still a novelty to Beth. They sit in a circle and talk about the countryness—trees, yes, look at all of them.

The partner and his wife have sons, too, around the same age, and so all the sons are expected to play with one another among the trees, that most basic social arithmetic. It's the companion equation to that of young Jewish fathers, who grew up with nothing, pointing at lot lines and planning all the things they will one day own. And young mothers cutting watermelon slices, saying nothing about themselves. Beth has already been shown the kitchen again, agreed again that such counter space is impossible to find in the city.

The four boys are running, and Beth sees Dave fall, coltish legs folding over a tree root like a wooden puppet suddenly abandoned by its master. She makes a little involuntary *oh* noise and takes a step toward her son, but before the worry can even peak, he's up, running to catch the others, pretending to fall again to make them laugh.

She calls to him anyway, at his back, "Honey, are you okay?"

He doesn't hear her and the words settle into the lawn. The other mother smiles at her, recognizing the impulse to worry for no reason. All of this, Dave's fall, his rise, the understanding smile of mutual motherhood, is to be expected. Beth knows that. It's relieving, or at least it's supposed to be, the notion that every role here is preordained. She is meant to over-worry and her son is meant to defy her fears. But Beth likes to worry, and this is where Josh does his looming.

A minute after Dave runs away from her calls, Josh materializes behind Beth's chair. She doesn't have to turn around to see him. She feels him linger. He's already nearly as tall as she is, taller now that she's sitting. He casts a shadow on her torso. Nothing needs to be said. A scene that was normal has been made not. There were four boys, feet clomping, and four parents, stationary, and Josh has made the numbers uneven, crowding in on the adults, already at the fraying edge of what should be a limitless tolerance for play.

My father is mid-sentence. He is always mid-sentence. He's talking about a movie, one that he swears they saw together, but Beth can't remember it. He's making loud and certain statements about this movie. He's saying something about how one cannot really *understand* this movie until one understands its influences. Beth must time her interjections. His words are like fan blades, and she is a little girl trying to stick her finger in the fan, pull it out before she feels a sting.

She says his name once, a whisper. Then once louder. Then almost a yell.

He doesn't turn his head toward her or their son still lurking. Only his eyes move, and they stab at Beth—*Could we please not have any fucking embarrassment? Just for an afternoon. Please?*

Beth pulls her eyes like a hitchhiker's thumb. *We need to leave. He needs to leave. He has been trying so hard for you to behave like he's having fun.*

Josh kneels on the deck and begins to wrap the cotton of her skirt around his fingers.

A full and vicious fight happens without any words or movements. Beth wants my father to look at their son. He won't. She is a nag. He is an asshole. Josh is fine. Josh is breaking. Beth looks down at her boy, now so close that he could rest his chin on her lap if he wanted to. He looks up at her. He is saying *please,* again and again. He is always saying *please,* though it's a word he never speaks out loud. A silent word keeps her awake into the early morning just in case, gives her a sense of purpose stronger than anything she's ever known.

"Fine," my father says out loud. And then to the hosts, "We're going. Apparently it's time to go."

That night my father sleeps, sunburned and snoring, and Beth watches him until it becomes clear that he will not open his eyes. Then she walks down the hall to Josh's room, past family photos that show no detail in the dark. She finds Josh awake, sitting up, feet tapping on the floor. He sees her looking through the doorway and stands. She begins to say something that might come out like an apology or at least an excuse for him—*It was so hot out there today; I think that wore us all down*—but all she manages is a short, wordless noise as Josh grabs a picture frame off his wall and holds it high above his head. He waits for her to say, "Don't," and then as soon as she does he throws it down with all his strength.

The smash isn't as loud as she expected. Shards of glass plink across the floor. Josh gives his greatest defender a defiant look. Beth goes to find a dustpan. She returns to kneel beneath him, ignoring the sting on her bare knees. She's done this before. The littlest shards catch in broom bristles, so she uses her cupped hand to scoop. She stretches for each sharp fragment. She won't let him cut his foot and bleed in the mess he made.

Years later, there's a drum set sitting on the same patch of floor where she once cleaned broken glass. It's not brand-new anymore, but Josh cares for it, and it's still cellophane-shiny. Josh is on the stool that came with the drum set, and he's smiling a full, real, mesmerizing smile.

"Play more," Beth is telling him. "Again. Can you do that exact same thing again?"

And he does it. He complies with her request, happy to do so.

The drum set was a birthday present, one of the last things that Beth and my father ever agreed upon and bought together. They gave it to him the morning he turned twelve, and both were too rapt, too hopeful, to give in to impatience when he spent the day beating on the cymbals, eschewing all rhythm in favor of sheer volume.

Then my father splurged on four good seats for *Dreamgirls* on Broadway, and they went as the kind of family Beth always wanted to have—father handsome and suited, sons near stoic, behaving as though they weren't overmatched by high society but rather born of it. Josh stared at the orchestra section, his feet tapping along with their sounds, and Beth smiled to herself as she planned how she might describe him to anyone who asked— *oh, he's our musical one.*

It was a moment so brief and perfect that Beth feels the need to prove and reprove its existence to herself. For two years, she has worked at quantifying his talent. Every day noise fills the apartment and still she asks for more. Play again, play louder. Her friends say she's something between a lunatic and a saint, but it's just the two of them in the apartment so often. My father is gone. Dave is out with friends, being a normal boy who wants nothing to do with his mother. There would be no sound at all if Josh wasn't providing it.

He messes up a little on a transition and says, "Shit, fuck."

She rushes to him. No it wasn't even a mess-up, she tells him. She couldn't hear anything wrong. Play it again.

"My little Ringo Starr," she says, sitting down on his bed. "My Ringo, it was perfect."

Ringo is the only drummer she knows.

"Ringo, what will you play for your mother next?" she says.

"Ma, stop it," Josh says, but it doesn't sound to Beth like there's much conviction in his voice. This is banter, for God's sake. Real, snappy, teenager-to-mom banter, the boy growing bashful the way he should, the mother pushing through the bashfulness, saying, *No way, mister, I'm not going to let you off the hook of my positive reinforcement.*

"Play it again for me," she says. "Please."

"It wasn't even anything, Ma. It was nothing."

It's never nothing. It's always something, and something new. Last week she paraded him in front of two neighbor ladies who had come over for afternoon coffee and a standard post-divorce checkup, though they never would have said it aloud. "How am I?" she said to them. "Come look at this, and you'll see how I am." Josh had been given a xylophone and sheet music by the percussion teacher at school, and he was dutifully staring at the squiggles on the page, forcing himself to play until a sound that was sophisticated and melancholy rang from the metal strips. It was a classical German song with an impossible name. He was making beauty out of something Beth couldn't even understand.

Beth clapped long and loud for him then, kept going after the neighbors stopped. She claps that way now as Josh relents and begins to play once more. She stays on the bed, leans in as though she can barely hear him. They are maybe two feet apart. If she wanted to, Beth thinks, she could reach out, cup his shoulder with her hand, and he would not shrug her off because he would be concentrating too hard.

The next morning, the fan is creaking in the kitchen and he hates her. That's how things go. He calls her a bitch while she makes him eggs and won't tell her why. She watches him eat in silence. She hates silence. He leaves the plate for her and stalks back to his room, and it feels like she can't breathe. All morning, she can't breathe. But at some point, finally, she hears music. She returns to his doorway, and there he is, talented and restrained, the way she loves to see him. He is concentrating all his energy on making something sound right. She walks to his bed and he doesn't tell her no. She asks him to play more.

Fifteen years later, none of the furniture has been replaced. Beth has accumulated new possessions, hasn't removed anything. The couch has picked up throw pillows to the point of being almost unsittable. The shelves have collected trinkets and now bow slightly in the middle. Being alone, it's comforting to pack in the open spaces.

Josh is home now, though, so home feels crowded. Beth doesn't know how long he plans to stay, but he's here and so she cares for him. He sleeps in his childhood bed, the one bought when he and Dave first got separate rooms. She checks on him at night, sock-shuffling on tiptoes to be quiet, gripping his door frame and craning her head, a movement that has returned effortlessly to her. He doesn't stare back like he did as a boy. He doesn't have the energy. Either he shivers and moans and stares straight at the ceiling or finally, mercifully, he sleeps. Beth is happy in these brief moments. She likes to watch him sleep.

He arrived a few days ago, unannounced. She hugged him and he went limp in her arms. They almost fell together. He didn't pull away, and though his sweat bled through cotton and felt itchy on her skin, it was a nice moment. He put his bag down next to her and walked to the bathroom. She stood outside the door and heard him vomiting, a sound both young and old. His voice was hoarse and tired when he moaned in between bouts. When he wasn't making noise, she asked if he needed anything, and he didn't respond. Sometimes he gasped, quick breaths, almost cute.

She worked up the courage to open the door, and he didn't tell her to get out. He looked up at her and nodded, which felt like thanks. She knelt behind him and ran her fingertips in circles between his shoulder blades, the spot that always made him coo as an infant. He let her. He was folded in front of her like a closed accordion. He was, for the first time in a long time, soft to touch.

She couldn't help but look at his arms. She'd never seen needle tracks before. They were little holes in him, and she thought if she put her ear up to them, she could hear air escaping. She wondered how long they'd been there. And then suddenly it was like they'd never not been there, all at once, that fast.

"There's meat loaf," she said. "Fresh. I was just making it."

He couldn't eat then. He couldn't eat for nearly two days. He could only puke and shake. But now he's a little stronger. Beth is heating up the leftovers in the microwave, and he smells the meat and pads out to join her in the kitchen.

"It's so nice to see you better," she says as she sets a plate in front of him.

He says nothing and takes a bite. She smiles as she watches him savor it.

"So how long are you planning to stay?" she says. "Now that you're strong."

She doesn't mean to pressure. She wants to know, that's all. What does he need? What can she do for him and how long can she do it for? He has been so gentle. He has been so willing to be helped, and that has made her greedy for more.

"Jesus, Ma," he says. "Don't worry about it."

"What, me, worry?" she says. She's trying to be funny, since she always worries, so she laughs a little to show him that she's joking. When he doesn't laugh with her, she says, "You know me. I'm a worrier."

"Well, stop," he says.

"I worry for *you*."

"Fucking stop."

"My—"

She hasn't measured the room since they moved in, so it's hard to say exactly how far his plate travels. At least ten feet, she has to figure, diagonally across the kitchen. She watches her meat loaf float past her head and then smash into the off-white wall— eggshell, the color is eggshell. It's a loud crash this time. It's the sound of a grown man who, no matter how weak he was a day ago, no matter how gentle, could kill her with thrown porcelain. It's not that she thinks he wants to, just that he can.

He walks out because that's how it's always been. He leaves her to clean. This time she weeps. She weeps for how many times she can be fooled. She weeps because when a boy feels small and afraid all you want to do is make him feel big and unafraid, and the moment he does he hates you for your effort. She should have thought these things before. Maybe she did, then forced herself to forget them. But now she's older and he's thirty and he's, apparently, a heroin addict, and it feels like the first time she ever thought that maybe she tried too hard to be nice.

Josh returns to the doorway to glare at her, but his face seems softer already, almost sorry. She pities him, even now.

"Ma," he says. "Ma, I told you to leave it alone."

"Josh—"

"You made me."

He walks away again. She kneels. She works over her floor with a sponge, rubbing with the coarse side, scooping up every bit of splattered beef, good meat that will never be eaten.

There is a last moment. It's not really the last one, but it's one that stands out, a break from their routine, almost nice, so it will live over and over again in Beth's mind. She doesn't know that yet. She just knows that he has returned for another detox and she can no longer remember how many times it's been. She spent years, his whole twenties, wanting him to come home. Now, too late, he seems nearly always present.

He enters with a cane and a shuffling limp.

"I'm like Richard the Third," he says, and Beth forces herself to smile.

It's the first time she's ever felt conscious of not just her son's impending death but how it might come, how he might look when it happens. As she watches him struggle to hang his coat in the hall closet, she feels liberated. There is nothing to worry about anymore because there is nothing that she can do. Maybe it was always that way. What a thing to think.

He offers information without her asking. The limp is from an infection. He put a dirty needle into the narrow band of skin between his big toe and the next one. It hurt like hell, he says, but his arm veins, those once-raised cables that Beth watched snake along his skin as he pounded his drums, are depleted.

"There's nothing left to shoot," he tells her, and he holds a wilted appendage up for her to see. She looks away.

Before she can ask, he says, "I haven't gone to the doctor. I know, I know, I'm sorry. I haven't been home for a while to call him."

She doesn't ask where he's been.

"I need to go home now, though," he says. "There are pills at home for the pain."

He pauses because the next bit is hard to say.

"I don't want to go alone. I don't think anything good will happen if I go alone."

She will take him. He wants to feel better, and she will help him feel better, watch the relief, impermanent but still sweet, move across his face. On any day before this one, she would have cycled through the logical questions that get a meat loaf thrown. What pills? Are they safe? How did you get them? Don't you think that maybe this could be an opportunity to get clean for real, cold turkey, to decide that this pain will be the end of it?

No more questions.

The subway has been running to Roosevelt Island for years, but they ride the tram because he wants to. He wants to fly over New York like a pigeon, too small and high up to be noticed, seeing everything. They sit side by side. Beth's shoulders, beginning now to slope and round, press against the skin just above her son's elbow. They get on the bus going downtown. They've never ridden this bus together. They are never in Manhattan together. They are hardly outdoors together. Beth goes to work, then back to her apartment. Josh moves around the city in dark places that she used to imagine and now is content to never see, returns home to her when he needs something.

It's rush hour for other people, and on the crowded bus they are beautifully anonymous, a mother and a son like any other, which, Beth thinks, is the full expression of all she has ever wanted for them. People jostle and mutter. People live lives and Beth watches. Then she has a funny thought. It's really funny, not just funny in her head but something to make him laugh, too.

"This is like *Midnight Cowboy*," she says. "I'm Jon Voigt and you're Al Pacino. With the limp."

She feels Josh shake as he laughs.

"It's Dustin Hoffman in *Midnight Cowboy*," he says. "But, yeah."

They're on a bus, like in the movie. They're heading south, not all the way to Florida but, still, south. And nobody else around them knows about his limp, about what they've seen, about what they're going to do.

Josh laughs again and says, "That's pretty funny, Ma."

She feels his warmth on her. They don't speak for the rest of the ride. They let their bodies lurch together in silence as the driver stops short and starts again. There are other things that she would like to say. There has to be something more than *Midnight Cowboy*, Josh as damaged hustler, Beth as loyal Texan gigolo.

They get off the bus, and he's all focus, walking ahead of her as fast as he can in his condition. She listens to his cane on the sidewalk and thinks of a scary story she was told as a girl, something she can't quite remember about an escaped psychopath and a *knock knock knock* sound. He fumbles with his keys in the door, rushes in, and starts digging through papers and old tissues, unopened mail in ominous, official envelopes. She sees him find the pills by the kitchen sink. Sees him sigh and try to turn away from her. Sees him pour them into his palm, sees him swallow, sees relief, will remember that look of relief.

Jamaica Kincaid wrote a memoir about her enigmatic younger brother who died of AIDS. It's a detailed portrayal, but her brother remains, appropriately, a hard character to see. He is most vivid when she describes her mother with him. When she describes the two of them together in the ocean near the end of his sickness, their images melding into a womb, into a horizon.

She writes: *He was swimming with my mother and they looked so beautiful, the water parted for them in ripplets, forming fat diagonal lines on either side of them, the two of them, one black, one gold, glistening, buoyant, happy just then, within speaking distance of each other but not speaking to each other at all.*

In the ocean, on a bus, mother next to broken son, like if she's peaceful and present all his fragments won't crumble apart. There's no closeness like that one.

I'm fidgeting and thinking about Jamaica Kincaid, watching Beth cry in her living room. She pantomimes Josh's relief. She closes her eyes, slackens her face, lets her shoulders sag in perpetual exhale. Like that, she tells me. I look past her out the window. Night has fallen. The river is black, and I can see Manhattan lights smudged on the water.

Beth ends her impression and shrugs.

"It's just, I felt so bad for him," she says. "I still do. Maybe there are people in the world who should get more pity, but for me, he was mine and I always pitied him."

She takes a breath and holds it in, deciding whether to say what she wants to say before she exhales. I grab a tissue box from the coffee table and hand it to her. The idea is to feel useful, but I think I just come off as condescending. When I sit back, the couch groans under me, a vulgar noise.

"When you came along," she begins, "I knew he was in trouble. That's all I remember for a while, is thinking of him and you. I didn't know what he might do to be heard. I think with boys, maybe the whole idea is that people listen to you. So I was going to listen to him. I thought *somebody* had to listen to him."

I'm quiet. I hold still. I have the strange feeling that if I move or speak, a well of emotion will rush out and I won't be able to plug the hole. I hadn't entertained this thought, this now obvious possibility that I belong in the same breath as all the things that enraged him, that closed in around him, that he wanted to break. Even as I worshipped him, it was not nearly enough to make amends for my presence.

Beth's cat leaps onto her lap.

"Hi, little girl," she whispers. The cat noses her fingers.

"She does yoga with me sometimes in the morning," Beth says. "No, really, you should see it. All the poses. That's our thing."

She smiles at me and then looks down at the coffee table, licks her thumb, and wipes the glass.

I am looming in a very different way than Josh used to in this apartment. There is the obvious looming—I'm so much bigger than Beth and all the collectibles that crowd around us—

but there's also something overbearing in the sheer audacity of my being here, my prodding her forward through each anecdote, asking her to tell me more about how it hurts. She lost her son to the holes he punched in himself, to the heart that he stopped while trying to feel relief. I am not dead and I need less relief. These are basic truths, maybe biological, maybe biographical. Luck, either way. I wonder if being the mother of Josh, if being the mother of any dead addict son, means that all live sons, young men who are strangers or kin, feel like they're taunting each time they look at you, clear-eyed, and say hello.

I don't know Beth as anything but a mother. She was doing it before I was born. She has worked at it, and I have seen the lines of that effort on her face, across Thanksgiving tables as she watched Josh try not to fall asleep. I have seen the strain in her eyes as they followed him out every door he exited. I remember the closeness of the two of them now, her gaze never off him, and I remember wanting to understand it, the unity of it, a twinship. Since he died, without realizing it, I've associated her mostly with that death, as though part of her has rotted and finally fallen off. How can every grown man not remind her?

Now I'm in his place on the couch where I was never meant to be, and he cannot pad back into the room to apologize.

"I remember one particular moment when it was just me and him talking," Beth says. "We were on this couch. We were as close as you and I are now. He goes: Yeah, Ma, Luke seems happy and good and loved and all that, but just wait a few years. Then the shit will hit the fan for him. He'll know he's alone. He'll be miserable."

She coughs and keeps going. "And I remember his voice. It sounded like he was really looking forward to that because things seemed so solid around you. And it didn't seem fair."

The talking stops here. I watch Beth as she breathes, watch

the skin around her clavicle ripple like running a spoon over the top of pudding.

I watch her but I think of a conversation I had with my father years ago. Josh had just left our place after a detox attempt. It was the first time he'd done it in front of us, but I never saw him. He was behind a closed bathroom door, and I had to settle on hearing him retch. My father took me to the park to shoot baskets. He didn't want to talk but I did. I remember being scared. I remember asking him, What if I get sick like that? If it's not his fault, then can it happen to me? Mostly, I remember the ease with which my father said no, how sure he was that I had no reason to be afraid of myself, as he caught my rebound, tossed me the ball, told me to shoot again.

I was assumed immune to that affliction, always. And always I've wondered if the assumption was the thing that kept me safe. Tell a child he is not one to lose himself, and when he's high on Vicodin, sad over a breakup, he will not reach for anything more. Tell a child he's fine, and he'll believe you. It cannot be that simple.

Beth tries to feed me Bagel Bites that have been in the freezer for a long time. I decline and she says *please*. I shouldn't go home hungry; that's not right. She hands me the food, wrapped in a paper towel.

I stand up and say, "Thanks."

She says, "I'm sorry," but I'm not sure what for.

I take the tram back across the river, an overthought homage to the stories Beth told me. The pod moves haltingly and groans in the wind. I'm afraid of heights, so I look at the floor. I imagine my brother and his mother up here, swaying into one another, together, close.

When I read Josh's notebooks, often I find myself abandoning all direction except the search for any acknowledgment of my presence. It's there. Only twice. Both mentions come from his dream journals, where he always believed he'd find explanations. The first is abstract:

[NOTEBOOK, UNDATED, "DREAM"]:
Last night, I went to bed and my "outside" was content. I popped a Xanax and this was supposed to carry me on my way. Dreams ate away at the little orange pill. Shame. Thinking of how pathetic I am. Dreamed that I should be working. Boss is calling me. I'm hiding. Under the desk. Porn magazines under the desk, Luke, a Chinese girl, whores. The inside rules.

I look for meaning in my company. Me, some porn, a Chinese girl who is not named, and more than one prostitute—we are the objects that he hides with. Or, we are the objects that manifest his shame. That glare out from his inside and remind him that he isn't who he wants to be. Or, we are toys, the kind that are soothing at first because you can see them as uncomplicated, but you always feel worse for having played.

The second mention is more direct:

[NOTEBOOK, UNDATED, "POWER DREAM"]:
I saw myself golden and huge. My father was standing in the shadows trying to talk to me, holding the baby. I looked at him and his baby; doomed.

I've stared at this one for a long time trying to figure out who he's talking about when he says *doomed.* My father and I in the shadows together? Him, golden, alone? All of us? There's nothing more about me, nowhere deeper to dig. And as a friend once told me: Write a dream; lose a reader. Because dreams are nothing but crossed wires unless you're hell-bent on looking for meaning. And forced meaning is cheap because then anything counts.

It feels good that he wrote of me, I know that. Even doomed, even under the desk, in the shadows, with all the things he no longer wanted to see.

I force myself to look out the tram window because I want something to do. In front of me are stacks of high-rises, Manhattan at its most overbearing. I think I can see people moving on a top-floor balcony. I have a realization that cannot be proved. That always, and especially the last time with Beth, Josh wanted to take the tram for this way of seeing. Here, you are not crammed next to people on the ground, not part of the street-bound tangle of legs and wheels. Here, floating, you're at the perfect height to see the tallest of what has been built, not the slow construction of it, not the base. And you can see figures in windows moving, not below you but in front of you, suspended in glass a hundred yards away. High up, so they must be happy, but you can't see their faces to confirm their happiness or feel less than them. You are moving and yet you feel still. You are suspended in possibility. You are, for ten minutes, over black water, comforted.

Beth is often present in his writing, more present than anyone. He always speaks of her gently, with regret or reverence or a promise to atone. In the same notebook, twenty pages later, but who knows how many months or years, there's a short poem written in blue ink, with looping, tired handwriting:

[POEM, UNDATED, "STAY"]:
Just look upon me (mother!)
Bless me. Do not go. Do not stay.
I will be here.

He was. And so was she. She still is.

. . .

I remember a lot of books in Josh's apartment, some borrowed from our father, some new. I remember him reading aloud because he liked the rhythm of a particular passage. I remember Post-it notes sticking out over spines. But when the boxes were brought home after his death there were no books to read from. A keyboard, a collection of Beatles sheet music, a lot of CDs, but I don't remember any books. In high school, I tried to teach myself to play his Beatles sheet music on his keyboard. I managed to get the left hand down on "Hey Jude," but then I quit, content to plod through the rhythm and sing until my voice cracked.

I don't know where the books went, or how present they really were. He did save writing, but only the kind that came in quick, unprofessional bursts. He saved his own work, of course, a decade's worth of it, and he also saved writing addressed to him. I think reading a novel, something fully formed and outside himself, became increasingly difficult. The addiction robbed energy and empathy equally. But he read and reread the scraps of loose-leaf that bore his name, that confirmed his existence, his address. He stuffed them into a plastic bag, knotted and unknotted until the handles broke.

Only one piece of correspondence is negative, and it's the last he ever received. It is so starkly out of place that I can only assume he didn't have time to throw it out:

YOU ARE HEREBY ORDERED to appear for a VIOLATION OF PROBATION HEARING at 9:30 a.m. on 06/02/2000 before judge A. GOLDBERG in part AA70 of the SUPREME Court of NEW YORK County.

This letter is dated May 19, 2000, a week before he was found. When I scan through the correspondence bag, it's always the first piece I read; then I quickly ignore its implications, the way he must have tried to do. It's a glaring question, one with an answer that he didn't want to see and that I'm not sure I want to know.

The rest of the documents, the ones consciously saved, are kind, praising. They span more than a decade and have been, I think, decisively curated, pared down to only the positive.

He kept each paper from college deemed worthy of an A, even a B+ in political science that showed promise. Red pen comments:

Comprehensive and thorough!

Well done!

Great work, but PROOFREAD!

He kept a response from a Brown education professor whom he mailed about a business plan that he developed and briefly got off the ground—a high school curriculum worked into rap songs that he wrote. The response is kind but curt, short enough to be almost a form letter. He highlighted the encouraging phrases in pink marker:

Wonderful Ideas.

Keep Trying and I believe you'll get there.

Respectfully yours.

Mostly, it's love letters, all kinds of love. I pour these out on my coffee table, read until they become the same:

It hurts when you yell at me. I want you to approve. If everything works out fine, I think we'll get married and have a family.

It feels so good to have somebody that I love.

I really mean it when I say that I will always be there for you.

Please return my kiss.

Consider yourself hugged!

You smell so good. You write such good letters. I am so lucky, I think.

Happy Birthday, you handsome dog.

You. Are. Still. My. Valentine. And you will be for a long time.
You are talented. You are unique.

I imagine him reading each letter, then carefully refolding. It seems like every missive is signed with a different name:

Love, Evelyn.
Forever, Grace.
Love you always, Nerrisa.
For now, Sonia.
Love, love, love, Anisha.
Booba.
Priya.
Sima.

She asks me to call her Sima because long ago my brother told her about a woman named Sima who he loved and missed. And it's nice to think about reminding someone of their love—less complex, less exposed than being loved all on your own.

This is the day she meets him:

She is working the counter at a sandwich shop on East Twenty-Sixth Street. It's the late 1990s. She arrived in New York only months before. She is twenty-five, both young and old for her age. At home, in a suburban community in Bangladesh, she had felt every bit of her quarter century lived. When she walked to the store for groceries, she knew everything to expect, each passing face running into the next, each with something to say that she'd heard before. When life is so predictable, it's as though you've lived it for a very long time.

Now Sima is young every day. She is a baby, practically, on the 7-train to work from Jackson Heights, way out in Queens, smelling piss and man-stink, unable in the rush-hour crowd to tell who is emitting what smell, unable to shuffle away. And she feels eyes on her, too. There are men, dozens of them in every train car, who stare at her so blatantly that their looks become fingers and she feels them poking up her calves and into the soft crease behind her knees and up her thighs and finally onto her rear, which she wishes, a pure, intense wish, would somehow deflate a little. Every day she crams herself into the clinging denim of the jeans she buys at the dollar store down the block from her apartment, walks to the train, and begins again.

Sometimes her mind blanks. Or not quite blanks but woozes, forgetting hours, snapping back into full consciousness when her boss yells or when the train door is about to close at her station, and that jolting sensation, more than anything, makes her feel like a child looking at the sky until boredom becomes the passage of time.

"Hello, you look very nice," she hears, and it brings her back from a wooze.

Before she even turns to put a face to the voice, she smiles. This is the first nice thing she's heard all day. When you're the one making sandwiches while others wait hungry, you don't often hear the best in people. Voices are snide and impatient; they make her not want to look up. This voice is soft. And there is something else, too, the realization climbing up her blushing face. Was that Hindi? Did a voice across the cold-cuts counter on Twenty-Sixth Street just speak kindly to her in Hindi? Her ears are confused. In this setting, they're trained to pick up and understand barked, rushed English. At home, there is Hindi, also barked, from family members and, sometimes, the man she is to marry, who is getting himself too comfortable with commands. Her worlds and their languages don't mix.

This Hindi accent is terrible, but the speaker is straining to sound right, and that's sweet.

She looks up.

"Hello," he says again, in Hindi. He smiles, a broad smile with big, flat teeth, and she feels herself keep smiling back.

It's a perfect scene, the two of them together for the first time, even under the fluorescent lighting that makes the sandwich cheese look radioactive. There are other customers scattered at fake marble tables, but they are obscured and irrelevant. Her fellow sandwich makers on the line don't look up; they mayo buns and grate iceberg like they always do. It's just Sima and Josh on opposite sides of a sneeze guard, smiling at each other.

There is silence as she tries to decide how to respond to him. She could attempt to flirt, toss his Hindi hello back in American slang. Or she could make a little joke about his accent, correct the way he fails to round his vowels. But, no, nothing flirty. She freezes, stays silent, and hides her smile with the back of her hand. He laughs and says hello again, this time as a question. She laughs at that and now they're laughing together.

He has a round head, with lots of extras on it. Extra skin, bloated circles climbing up from his neck. A beard with gray flecks, coating the fat. He's sweating, and individual beads cling to his beard hair. He raises a thick hand to his face to wipe off the moisture.

He looks so sheepish and unaccustomed to his frame that Sima can't help but speculate about how he once looked, what has been lost. His whole torso is shrouded in a wool coat, green-and-blue checked, like a lumberjack from an air-freshener commercial, very American. It's hot today. Everyone else is in T-shirts.

He orders a turkey sandwich. She makes it for him and they talk. It's just pleasantries, little snippets of chatter about the weather and the crowd in the shop, different types of cheese. She wants more. She wants to ask him why he's wearing a wool jacket on such a nice day. She wants to ask him how he knows Hindi. She wants to ask him what's wrong because there does seem to be something wrong, a wince on his face even as he smiles, a throb, hard to explain, in his brown-green eyes. She wants to ask him why he spoke to her, why that small decision feels already like it matters.

A month later it's even warmer and he's back in the shop still wearing that jacket. It's the lunchtime rush, and he is the only customer not hair-gelled and preppy, with shiny loafers that clack as they shuffle down the line. Sima thinks it's strange to see a white man not shrouded in office attire.

It's Josh's turn to order. She prints his ticket and tries to keep her eyes down on the condiment buckets.

"It's me," he whispers to her in Hindi.

Obviously. Before she can answer, he says, "May I have your number?" again in Hindi, a secret that nobody else in the shop can intercept. His accent is getting better. He comes in so often now and he practices with her. Sometimes he doesn't even buy a sandwich, he just stands and talks and then eventually says good-bye.

Sima's mother's voice is clear in her head, a firm and pursed *no* to everything this burly stranger is offering. She has a job that she should be grateful for that he is distracting her from, a future husband back in Queens who she should be far more grateful for. These are things she knows rationally.

She is lonely.

She scribbles fast on the back of his ticket, and he holds it up like he just won something.

"Thank you," he says.

She smiles and tries to go back to work.

He leans over the sneeze guard and says, "I'm going to call tonight. Can I call tonight? Please?"

There are many concerns to consider, primarily that when her future husband is around, he always picks the phone up first. But tonight he's working and Sima will be alone, staring out her barred window at all the people pulsing along the avenue below who don't know her and never will.

The suits stuck on line behind Josh are growing restless, and Sima feels their glares, eyes like fingers again, poking.

"Sweetheart," one says. He points to the face of his watch.

"I'm going," Josh says. "But I'm calling. Tonight, I'm calling. Unless you say no, I'm calling."

The rest of the day is wooze. The rush ends, then comes the late afternoon drag, then she's home alone and nothing worth stopping for and really experiencing happens until the phone rings.

His voice sounds like he's been crying.

"Are you okay?" she blurts out in English, hearing her own stilted accent echo back at her through the fuzzed connection. "Is there anything I can do for you? What's wrong?"

He says, "Nothing," and she can picture his face pleased that she asked. What a funny thing, to know someone's expression when you can't see them. Outside her window, trucks thud in the potholes on Northern Boulevard.

"Where *are* you?" Josh says into the phone.

"It doesn't matter," Sima says. "Where are you?"

She wraps her fingers around a mug of tea, listens to Josh breathe, and tries to picture where he might be. Where would a man like him live? She thinks of the borough of Manhattan, long and pinched the way it's drawn on subway maps, full of shimmering surfaces with white faces reflected in them. She pictures a tall building, all black glass. He is in some apartment, somewhere in those black windows, but she cannot muster any detail around him. Just his face, smiling, sad.

"It doesn't matter," he says. "Tell me about your life. Please. I want to know."

———

Maybe, after all the long talks, she asks him outright what his demon is or if there are many of them. Maybe he just volunteers the information at some point because he senses that she wants to know. Often she can't remember how their conversations begin and is hardly conscious of when they end because they pick up again days later, so fluid each time. There is always something at his edges, though, gnawing in at him, causing him to stop mid-story, right before the climax or the explanation, to say that there are things beyond his control. She wants to know more, to know all of him, and finally he lets her.

He's leaning at her over a small table near the back of the sandwich shop after her shift. His fingertips, bracing his weight on the table, almost touch hers, and she thinks about how she could give a sharp exhale and blow the stringy hair off his forehead. That's how close they are.

"I am good," he says. "That's what I've been saying. But there's this monster. Really, that's what it is."

He looks young, little-boy frustrated. He reaches his fingers forward to touch hers. She doesn't pull away.

"I can't not do it," he says. "You don't know about drugs. This is the thing: It's like I'm not allowed to not do it."

She nods for him, unsure and unconvincing. He is sallow under the fluorescents.

"I want to quit," he says. "Trust me. Do you trust me that I'm telling the truth?"

She does.

"There's a devil on my shoulder. The drug is the devil. I'm not the devil"—he pauses here because this is a crucial point to get across—"I'm not the drug. But the drug is right there, always. Always."

She holds his hands. He lets them go limp as she holds them and they look almost dainty. She has the realization that she might be the only person in the world who gets this close to him anymore, that this closeness is crucial. She wonders about the last time somebody not her looked at him like this, leaning forward, never backing away. Who was that person? When did that person stop leaning in? She tries very hard not to blink because that doesn't seem right. She looks down at his arms; he's left them bare today. He lets her see the shallow holes and ruddy irritations that spread like a constellation across his skin.

She has never been anything but sober, doesn't understand the mechanics of any type of high, and Josh loves that about her. Often he asks her to remind him of her forever sobriety, always responds with, *Amazing, you're amazing.* The holes in his arms make her think of the drug as alive, digging.

She runs the tip of her thumb across one of the needle tracks. He flinches, but then he lets her.

"It's important to me that you believe that I used to not be like this," he says. "I was crazy strong. Like feel-my-muscles strong. I wrote music. I can play you tapes. I owned this business. I told you that."

It's in Sima's nature to believe. She tells him, of course, asks him to show her that picture again, the one from when he traveled to India. He's standing against a graffitied wall, tan and beaming, with his shirt sleeves rolled all the way up to his shoulders, arms clean.

He thanks her with such force that they both fall silent. Then he decides to shift. She loves this about him, loves this the most maybe, his capacity for self-resurrection right in front of her, with their conversation hardly stalling. He sits up straight and waves his hand in between their faces, erasing what has been there. He says, *Hey,* like a dare. *Hey what?* she counters. She lets her torso stiffen along with his.

"Let's talk about *India*," he says.

So they do.

He's good at talking. He makes words do exactly what he wants them to, like he's building something and she's watching. The settings are lush when he describes them, the dirt neon orange, not brown, each person a vivid, almost glowing version of humanity. She's from there, and it never seemed as remarkable when she lived it.

He speaks about the past and then skips right to the future. The future is just as tantalizing as the past. Forget the present. The present is dull gray. The devil is heavy on his shoulder in the present. And her shoulders are heavy, too, weighted a little more with each subway ride and ketchup refill and silent dinner. In the present, she has one friend, this man sitting in front of her, talking about what has been and what might be.

"I've told you why India is the most beautiful place in the world, right?" he asks.

Yes, he has. "Maybe. I don't think so. Tell me."

The second time he went to India, he was alone, he tells her. He just bought a plane ticket and went because he couldn't stay away from the beauty. He had one backpack with him, that's it. Every morning he walked through Bombay to the same fruit stand to buy a mango from this tiny kid with an oversized smile. Never has anything tasted better than that mango tasted, and the kid watched him eat and he kept saying, *You like? You like?* All the children were so sweet. Fundamentally kind, even when they realized he couldn't give them much beyond high fives. He gave them all high fives. They said, *Howdy Partner*, like how they thought Americans did, and it made him laugh every time. No other place in the world is kind like that.

He's a tangle of words. Sima grins and he stops for a moment to watch her show her teeth. She looks down at her hands and then back up again, at him.

"We could go," he says, as she knew he would. "Just buy a

ticket. We could go now. Or tomorrow. Do you miss that part of the world? Do you miss home? I'll take you back."

He nods his head, urging her to do the same. She sighs and complies.

There is, there has to be, an unspoken recognition between them that they will never go to India together. Imagine if they tried. There would be a moment in his apartment when his decision would be simple—leave the drug and instead take India, take Sima, or keep everything the same. Yes, Sima is a believer, but not so much that she thinks she would win. And what of her own life? There's no leaving and returning on her delicate temporary visa. And even if she could, what would the conversation be in Jackson Heights as she packed? *I am going. I have to go. I need to live this moment with this man so I can feel something different. Yes, a man. He is my friend.*

Outside the shop, a taxi's honk is followed by the sound of a heavy fist beating on the hood. There is yelling.

"It will be none of this," Josh says, jerking his thumb toward the noise. "We'll wake up and we'll go play with the children. We'll eat mangoes. Do you remember how they taste?"

"Yes," she says. Yes for him. "They taste so sweet like they're still alive. We should go in May. Do you know they're juiciest in the spring?"

Both of their heads are still nodding. Not at the same time, but in sequence. She bobs up as he drops his chin down, like they're connected, pulling one another forward. He is imagining the mangoes. He is imagining her eating the mangoes, juices running down her neck, tropical sunlight on her black hair. She knows he is. She thinks that his imagination works harder than anyone else's. She told him that once. She said she thought he did drugs because his imagination was brighter, louder, more constant than any normal person's. She could tell he liked it when she said that.

"When we go, maybe it will be what I need to change," he says. He grabs a sugar packet from the table and shakes it in a rhythm. "I mean, Jesus, there will be beauty everywhere. New experience. Who needs a high then?"

Sima still doesn't know exactly why anyone needs a high in the first place.

"Yes," she says. "You'll be better."

Josh coughs and she watches every part of his body shake. The layer of fat around him bounces. His head swivels on his neck, a surprised look on his face like he hadn't realized how long the cough would last or how hard the next breath would be. He gives a shamed smile. Sima doesn't like to look at him when he doesn't want her to. She turns and watches two of her coworkers on a cigarette break, spitting heavy globs onto the sidewalk.

Suddenly, his palm is on her face. It's not an aggressive move, but, still, a lunge to caress her, his fingertips tugging at the thin hairs on the back of her neck. Soft hands, no calluses, no texture. He wants her. He makes a noise, no words, just a low grunt. She feels his thumb slide down, touch her bottom lip. Nobody has ever done that to her, touched her lip like that. It doesn't feel right that he's the one to do it. It's a present and physical act, his hand snatching, very real and very desperate.

"No," she says. She grabs him by the wrist, not hard, just enough for him to feel it.

She is relieved that he's gentle when she says no.

"I'm sorry," he says.

"I love you," she says, surprised at how blunt it sounds, how true it is. "I love you, but this is not us."

They exist together only as what they want to be and what they were. That's the gift that they give each other. Josh looks at Sima, his eyes wet and red. He places his hands, palms down, back on the table.

"We don't have to go to India," he says. "You already know

that part of the world. Paris. I can't believe you've never seen Paris. I want to show you Paris."

He means it. She is overwhelmed by how much he means it. She asks him what the Seine looks like at night so he has the chance to describe it. He tells her it's like living inside starlight.

When he calls late, she snatches the phone up midway through the first ring so that nobody wakes up. When she whispers hello, he says, I love you, I love you, and that is enough. He's breathing heavy into the line.

"I pray for you," she whispers into the phone.

It's true, and why should care be a secret? She wants good things for his soul; that is nothing to hide. And he is speaking slowly, breathing heavily enough to let her know that he is way too high to squabble with her about God. When he's sober, he likes to ask her what could possibly make her think that there is something strong and good up there, something that cares about us. Then she says, How could it not be so? And he says, Prove it, over and over until he gives up and they both start laughing.

She hears a happy sigh into the phone, his tongue muffling the sound.

"I do," she says. "I pray for you every night."

She imagines him with his eyes closed, savoring.

"You know there are only three people I really love," he tells her. She waits for him to say it. "I love you because you love me. You forgive me. You, Sima. And my mother. And Luke. I like the way you all look at me."

A week earlier, Sima met Josh's mother. She felt like a teenager then. Josh ushered Beth into the shop, and on her break they sat around a table, Josh saying, *Isn't she pretty? Isn't she sweet?* Beth answering, *Yes, yes.* She watched Beth squeeze his hand and look at both of them with hope. She even said something like, *I can't wait to see what comes next,* and Sima smiled and Josh smiled, and they sat around the table, none of them relenting and giving the true answer: nothing. Josh said he felt surrounded by goodness.

"I just want to be looked at that way," he says now. His breathing makes her throat hurt thinking how hard it must be to breathe like that.

"That's nice," Sima says.

He doesn't respond. She listens to the weighted silence of him nodding off, finally says his name, gently, like he's a little boy and it's morning. He comes back to her, a sharp inhale and then a cough.

"Hi," he says. "Hi, I'm here. I've been here."

"I can't believe you've never been to Paris," he says, forcing out the final *s* sound, slurring it.

"No, Josh, I never have."

It's a while before he talks again.

"It's so beautiful," he says finally. "The lights at night. You'll love it so much. You'll see. It will be so . . ."

She presses the receiver to her ear, willing him to finish. She wonders what a mind on heroin dreams. She hopes it's a better dream than her panicked sober dreams, jolts of warning until she wakes up, then instantly forgettable. She hopes that it's a luscious continuation of his last waking thought, that it's easy and warm. She tries to see it with him, the two of them in Paris at night. All she knows to imagine is the Eiffel Tower lit up, a snapshot from a package of postcards. She and Josh are together at the base of this image. They have nowhere else to be. They linger. Light shines on her face, and he looks at her, and he smiles, content, until the dial tone and then silence.

———

"Have you been to Paris?" she asks me.

I tell her I have. The first time, I was young, too young to remember much. Josh was there; it was his first time in Paris, too, a trip he told her about many times, six days of basic tourism. It was me, my mother, my father, and Josh in a little apartment that smelled like jam that my parents swapped for.

"I knew you were there," she says. "I don't know why I asked you. I knew that."

I try to hide how happy it makes me that she knew. It shouldn't be such a big deal. I'm still reveling in the fact that I was spoken of, that he said my name to her when he spoke of love. We're working together here, in our memories. She asks if I remember anything at all from the trip. I do, I say. A little. All I remember is him. I tell her that, and it makes her smile like fingers are pulling her lips back at the edges. She nods, my cue.

I remember buying a gargoyle in a gift shop, a monkey-man with wings and fangs, baring those fangs, crouched. I remember Josh doing an impression of a gargoyle. We were sitting on stone steps, under a stone building that I only remember as old. He had his leather jacket on, or I made that part up. He was leaning over me, baring his fangs the way gargoyles do it. He was making a hissing noise like a snake, and his lips were stretched so wide that I saw the base of his teeth pushing through his gums. I was laughing.

I remember sitting in the apartment, scared of the sound the radiator made when we turned the heat on. It was snowing outside, maybe. We were watching the only video available, *Who Framed Roger Rabbit* dubbed in French. Josh was pretending to be Jessica Rabbit, slinking around the living room, hands caressing his own neck, lips pouted, eyes nearly closed. *Bonjour,* he said, and I was laughing.

I remember visiting Jim Morrison's grave. I stood back and

watched. Josh knelt among the flowers and handmade signs, the poems and rain-warped packs of Marlboros. He was crying. I had no idea who Jim Morrison was, but I liked the visuals— the ancient green trees, the once-bright roses lying scattered. When we left, Josh said he wasn't crying out of sadness. He was, instead, awed by how loved the man had been, how indelible, fresh proof of his worth laid out with each arriving tour bus.

"Yes," Sima says when I relay the last memory. "He was going to take me to the grave. That was very important. He had a poet's soul."

I don't cringe at the phrase, though I feel the tug to do so. *Poet's soul.*

On the way back from the grave, Josh put his headphones on me and played "Back Door Man" on cassette. I don't tell Sima that part.

She has dressed for this occasion. Everything on her is starched—black slacks, white blouse, unbuttoned argyle cardigan. Her hair is pulled into a bun, and I look at her neck, its sloped sides. This is job-interview attire, clothing you can't breathe in. I wonder if she works in an office now. I don't ask. She has told me almost nothing about her present, only that she has a daughter, and she looked guilty when she showed me a wallet picture—a kid on class photo day; I can't think of anything else to say about it.

A decade has passed since she knew my brother. Most of her life in America has been spent without him, and so much can change for a person who seeks change. Sima is forward momentum personified, I know that even without filling in the details. I don't want to think about what she has accomplished since he finally couldn't manage breathing. I have a suspicion that if I prodded her through her modesty, I would get to a tale of employee-of-the-month plaques, incremental promotions, night school, the kind of resolute working motherhood referred to with folksy admiration at the beginning of politicians' speeches. But I don't want to ask for the specifics of how she thrived without him—I only want to know what she lost.

I ask if *she* has ever been to Paris because I know she'll say no.

"That was for us," she says. "It's expensive. And it takes time. That was a place for him to show me. Paris was his promise to me."

Promise is as generous a word as *poet*. What is a promise that is made without a chance of coming true, other than a lie?

I will take you.

I will be better.

We will be together.

There is a place, Paris, that's far from here, and lights glow off the river like lanterns floating in the sky.

"You didn't believe him, did you?" I say.

There's an undeniable scoff in my voice. I feel cruel. She half-smiles without showing her teeth and tilts her face down.

"I'm sorry," I say.

"I didn't believe that we would go," she says, with quiet emphasis. "But I believed in him. I believed that he thought we would. He was not a liar. He was a dreamer."

He was an addict. Maybe the difference is just semantic.

After talking with Sima, every time I revisit his writing, I will think of her. Because no matter what notebook I pick up, as I flip through pages of detox journals and poems and lists of self-affirmations, so many versions of the *REASONS TO GET CLEAN* heading, I will see the word *Paris* appear, punctuating his thoughts, a refrain that never ends.

[LOOSE-LEAF, OCTOBER 1998, "REASONS"]:

– *Because it is harder every time.*

– *Get your body back!*

– *It's either <u>success</u> or <u>this</u>.*
– *Mom is gone. Dad is gone.*
– *I can do three days. It's just three fucking days. A week. I can do a week.*
– *Remember, Paris in January.*

[LOOSE-LEAF, UNDATED, "UNTITLED"]:
What it means, is that I will not lose because I can't. The main thing is that I have an agreement with myself that if I have this (methadone) I will succeed. They will be in tandem, my methadone and my inspiration. They will not compete. Accomplished men say, "I couldn't have done this without my wife," etc. SAME THING. In two months, I will be in Paris at night. Two months. Paris.

I see the word repeated at the end of a sentence: *Paris Paris Paris Paris.* Or it's capitalized, *PARIS,* towering over all the little words around it. Or it's the last word written for a while, butted up against blank lines until finally lucidity returns and he begins again with, *I was gone too long.* Coming at the end of sentences, paragraphs, lists, it is often scribbled loosely, and I imagine a hand beginning to let go before the panic or the high, mostly the high, swallows all language.

Comforting feels like the wrong word, but, yes, it's comforting to think of him rushing to write *Paris,* to put it in pen, uneras-able, before the nod takes over, the same way he managed to say it to Sima on the phone before the line went silent. And Paris itself, what he knew of it, was the perfect word to say. A place ideal and far away. Just real enough to be a good hypothetical. A place that can exist in collective cultural imagination, free of urban sprawl and supermarkets and traffic congestion, just lights and river, the Eiffel Tower, good bread. A place to love and make art. I like to think that, above all, that's what he wanted to do.

In college, I traveled to Paris with Sofia, and we watched

children push miniature schooners in the pond where every-one watches children do that. I was running out of my parents' money, so we pretended to be the kind of kids who had to worry about such things, bought a single fresh baguette in the morn-ings, ripped off hunks all day as we walked until we were lost, talked about how we needed nothing more than this. It was exactly as those moments in a life are supposed to be—better than the moments around them, indulgent, brief, Facebook-logged, and then mostly forgotten.

I read Hemingway, of course, and got really into that whole possessive thing: *You belong to me and all of Paris belongs to me, and I belong to this notebook and this pencil.*

I read James Baldwin's Paris writing, too, and loved the swirl-ing emotion—relief, guilt, longing: *My flight had been dictated by my hope that I could find myself in a place where I would be treated more humanely . . . where my risks would be more personal, and my fate less austerely sealed. And Paris had done this for me: by leaving me completely alone.*

Baldwin showed up in Paris on the run, wanting to be some-body without history. And Paris, its specifics, didn't matter, only that Paris was not the place that he was running from. I saw Josh in cafés when I read Baldwin, anonymous to everyone but me, reborn clean. If there was anyplace for there to remain an ember of him, the promise of his life still pulsing orange, finally free from all back home that had tried to stamp him out, this was it.

Of course it was a stretch to find Josh in Baldwin because Bald-win was running from hatred and oppression, from unavoidable violence crashing in on him. Addiction is a very self-imposed brand of oppression, but still, it's better to think of the addict as oppressed than wallowing. Oppression doesn't carry inward blame. That has always been the hardest part of remembering him, the effort not to blame. The effort to believe that he fought it, even if it was him and whatever *fought it* means. To believe that if he had the chance to start over, it wouldn't happen again. Belief.

"I feel that he is alive now, still," Sima tells me. She leans across the table and her hands almost touch mine. "His spirit, I mean. He is watching us. I believe that."

I say nothing, so she says, "Maybe I sound cuckoo?"

It's not a question that I want to answer. Because yes, she does. I am not a believer. I was not raised for that. Neither was Josh, but I think he wanted to believe. In the end, he had to believe.

There isn't a language of addiction that takes atheism into account. The NA meetings that Josh quit, the Al-Anon groups my father later tried to find solace in—both required a relinquishing of control to that higher power that wants what is best for us. And really to believe what an addict tells you, tells himself, requires a predisposition for, or at least some experience in, faith. All you have seen is deterioration, but you are being promised regeneration, asked to trust that there remains some divinity, and despite how wholly unbelievable that is, you must believe. There's a reason why Sima was his last friend, the last he made and then the last to stick around. Why she is the only person I've found who knew him as only an addict. She never got to hear him play music, she never read his words, she never saw the muscle lines that ran like shadows across his torso. She only knew a man afflicted, making promises. Even that first time he spoke to her in Hindi in a sandwich shop on Twenty-Sixth Street, she knew something was wrong. He was waiting to be redeemed, and she never let herself say that it wouldn't happen. What a sap, I want to think, believing in the unproven and unlikely.

"No," I hear myself say. "Not cuckoo at all."

"I talk to him sometimes," she says. "I smell him, like he's sitting down next to me. Do you remember how he smelled? I remember how he smelled and how he spoke to me. I speak back."

I wipe my palms on my jeans, and I hear myself reciprocate with the last promises that Josh ever spoke to me. They may have been the last words he spoke to anybody, two nights before he was found. He called looking for our father, but I was the only one home. I was ready to hang up, but he said, "Wait, let's talk, let's tell each other about next year."

He talked about baseball because he knew that's what I liked. He told me I would be the star of my high school team, even as a freshman, and he would be standing there watching my exploits on a field in the middle of Central Park, fingers wrapped around the chain-link fence. I would hit a home run, and he'd be there, clear-eyed, real, cheering for me as I crossed the plate.

He never liked baseball. And the notion of his spectatorship as the ultimate redemption, like he was some divorced dad leaving a meeting early to make sure I saw him in his rumpled suit before my last big at bat, didn't make any sense. But I didn't think that then. He would be there. Absolutely, and the world around us would take on fuzzy, Kevin Costner–ish tones, two brothers reunited, cradled in the soft light of sober American nostalgia.

"Do you believe me?" he asked.

He was alone. I knew that. I listened for a sound in the background, anything. It was a hot night, and I think his windows were open. I could hear the tree outside his building, leaves scraping against brick. The dose that killed him must have been at hand, on the coffee table in front of him, maybe. I remember that he didn't want me to hang up the phone.

"Do you believe me?" he said again.

I said yes, and then he said good, and when there was nothing else we could say he was gone.

"Beautiful," Sima says. "That's beautiful."

She has to leave me soon, to visit her ailing mother, then pick up her daughter from her after-school program, then home for dinner, then straight to bed. But she will find time in between, she tells me, to light a candle for Josh, the way she did after his funeral. She won't tell her husband or her daughter, because they don't know who Josh is, was, and she doesn't want them to. When explained, he is dangerous, and the two of them together are sordid.

I will have dinner with my father tonight, and we'll sit under a wall of pictures of Josh's face, but none of them will look like the man Sima knew. We stopped framing him, not intentionally, I don't think, but because the pictures became more sporadic near the end, and anyway it seems like a disservice to loved ones to emphasize the fattest, most vacant-eyed versions of them. There's a picture on the wall from Paris, in a courtyard somewhere. I am in it; he is in it; we're posing. He is posing in every picture. These images, never spoken of, hang over every cup of coffee my father drinks, every morning newspaper he reads. When he looks up, they must sneer at him, before-shots, reminders of what was lost.

We'll talk about movies and deem most of them bad. He'll ask me how I'm liking my job, and I will say something ridiculous about how it feels like my very soul is being dragged out of my open mouth each time I sit at that desk. He will give a short smile. He will say that it's amazing how quickly time passes. Eventually he'll fall asleep to NPR whispering in the background, and I'll leave.

There is another Baldwin piece I love, and it has nothing to do with Paris. "Sonny's Blues" is about a Harlem man with a junkie, jazz-musician brother. It's about trying to listen. There's a scene where the brother is at the piano, playing, striving to make the narrator understand. Finally, for a moment, he does. Baldwin writes: *While the tale of how we suffer, and how we are delighted, and how we may triumph is never new, it always must be heard. There isn't any other tale to tell, it's the only light we've got in all this darkness.*

Josh is still speaking to Sima because that's what an addict is always trying to do, trying to tell you. Tonight, in Queens, in an apartment with barred windows and a steep mortgage, where there are no pictures of him, he will speak. Tonight, in a quiet, candlelit bedroom, he will tell her and she will listen, his voice filling her as she watches her daughter, a smiling child who has never done anything wrong, who likes to dance on the bed in her mother's skirts.

· · ·

Sometimes my father comes out to Brooklyn, and we play tennis on the public courts at the tail end of Prospect Park. Then he follows me through my neighborhood to my apartment. We have discussions on these walks that feel like they're designed for extra meaning—father and son treading on sturdy, well-practiced masculine clichés that make gravitas come easily. We are holding athletic equipment. We smell of sweat.

I tell him about my neighborhood.

He tells me how it used to be.

On my block, a young woman pulls one child with each hand, while another stumbles behind her. She stops and turns to the stumbling child, says, "Keep up, or I swear to *God.*" The child begins to cry and then rubs his eyes with tiny, balled fists. She says, "Stop crying, or I swear to *God.*"

I make an involuntary noise, a horrified half gasp. I'm thinking of the absolute exhaustion of being followed around by three small, helpless humans, compelled to love each of them fully and equally.

My father says, "What?"

I say, "I know you're supposed to fall in love when you see your child born, but still."

He says, "I always thought that was bullshit."

The woman in front of us hears the word *bullshit* and turns fast, wraps all of her children in her arms and hurries them away from us, happy, I think, for something concrete to protect them from. My father laughs and says, "When they're little, you're just trying to keep them alive. I don't think that's love. It's only love when they do stuff that makes you think about something other than keeping them alive. They get older. They say something funny. You can throw a ball with them. That's love."

Our rackets swing side by side as we walk.

It's hard to think about father-and-son relationships without feeling like everything is oversimplified. When I ask my father for a memory of Josh, he talks of a Little League game and then groans. He says, "Damn, I wish I said something better." But he didn't, so we start talking about Little League because Josh once played Little League, and after him I played it with more success, and before him my father played stickball in a parking lot in Coney Island.

Fatherhood is not meant to be unique; that's the point. The transactions are meant to be so smooth that they are unseen, a narrative that just exists, that nobody had to work to build.

On a nice new field by the river on Roosevelt Island, my father wears a windbreaker that says "Assistant Coach" and Josh runs like an animal that was never meant to run.

My father watches his son trace a course to his position in

deep right field. He wonders what possesses somebody to stick his ass in the opposite direction of where he's trying to go. Like, evolutionarily, what is that?

Josh stops by the fence and looks down at his feet.

My father paces the dugout in his windbreaker and tries to think of something that coaches say. He signed up for this gig because that's what young fathers do for their firstborns, but he's spent most of the season feeling fraudulent. The head coach, an Irish homicide detective who looks exactly like what he is, yells to the team with a voice born to command.

"Look alive, boys."

"We need this, boys."

None of the boys question the stakes. And they do look alive, caricatures, almost, of aliveness, a homogeneous gang of Liams and Patricks and Ryans, bouncing on their toes, waiting for a chance to dive and then rise again, filthy and triumphant. In the distance, at the base of the right-field fence, Josh doesn't hear anything.

Wind hurtles off the river. Josh looks cold. He rubs his ungloved hand on his bare arms and gives a little dance. The boys in the infield look like they couldn't possibly think of coldness at a time like this. My father wants to run out and drape a jacket over Josh's shoulders. My father doesn't want his son to be cold. But then he resents that impulse and resents the root cause of it, Josh, who could make the whole situation better simply by not behaving like a fawn lost in a snowstorm when in fact he is just a right fielder on a breezy April afternoon. My father is guilty for thinking this and then angry for being made to feel guilty, and the emotions continue to swirl like they usually do until he's jarred by the ping of metal bat on ball.

It's hit well, and by some absolute miracle of Little League physics, it's hit to right field. The game is tied and this is the last inning, and there's Josh weaving like a drunk toward a would-be game-winner. Every person on the field and in the bleachers is watching him. My father is aware of that. Grass crunches under Josh's cleats. The ball begins its descent. My father hears someone say, *Ah shit,* behind him, in preparation for a certain drop, maybe even a potential injury. Boy and ball and eyes end up at the same spot.

The catch is very accidental. Josh is frozen, legs splayed, hands up. His eyes aren't just closed, they're clenched so tight that the effort lines his face, visible even from so far away. But there's the ball nestled into his mitt, a true, unerasable success.

My father claps his hands until they sting. He paces the fence as he claps. He yells as loud as he can, "That was amazing. I said you could catch. Goddamnit, I *told* you."

He's never been this loud at a Little League game. He is overwhelmed by how loud he's being. He feels like someone not himself and he's momentarily embarrassed, but then he thinks he should be loud while he's got a reason to be. He has spent so much of Josh's childhood worried about the boy's fragility. He has said, "It's all right, you're all right," so many times—why not be loud in a moment that is better than just all right? Josh deserves to hear him like this. It feels good to hear himself like this.

When the game ends, my father's face is sore from smiling. He drapes his arm around his son's shoulder and he squeezes.

"You see?" he hears himself. "What did I tell you?"

And then, whispered, a conspiracy between the two of them, "What did I *fucking* tell you?"

They leave the field together. On the walk home, Josh is quiet. My father is willing this moment not to end. He's rehashing the catch out loud, and the catch grows more epic and untrue in each version. Josh looks up at him. He has beautiful eyes. There's no other word for them. They are brown but full of other colors. They change in the light. They are pure green sometimes, and sometimes orange, sometimes gray. My father wants to tell him that he notices all the colors, that he thinks they're beautiful. He remembers the way women used to crowd around the stroller and coo. How they'd say, "Those eyes. Oh my God, those eyes never end. It's like he *knows* something."

"Please, stop it," Josh says. "It's not a big deal."

It shouldn't be a big deal. It isn't. My father squeezes his son's shoulders, relishing the closeness until Josh says he can't breathe and wriggles away. They both fall silent.

He is seventeen now, and he's seventeen the way twenty-five-year-old heartthrobs are seventeen on TV. My father is watching him work out. They're alone in a fluorescent gym in the basement of the Roosevelt Island co-op. The pool is just outside and everything smells of too much chlorine. My father is sitting on a stool. Josh is lying on his back, heaving a bench-press bar up above his head and grunting so loudly that it's almost obscene. He isn't wearing a shirt. Muscles move like pistons as the bar rises and falls. My father wonders where all the muscles came from so quickly. He thinks that they shouldn't fit. Eventually, he has to burst, right?

Josh has printed a workout sheet so that my father can follow along with his movements. My father said, *Very professional,* when Josh handed him the sheet. He meant it, but he said it in a shitty way, and Josh didn't like that, and now my father feels bad.

"Are you watching?" Josh snaps at him.

He slams the bar back into place, springs up, then drops himself onto the floor for push-ups, narrates the precision in each movement. His voice is deeper now, but not so much so. It's still him. There's still a wavering quality to it. The voice doesn't fit the body anymore, and my father supposes that's the point.

"*Watch* me," Josh says. "Like actually watch."

He's up again, bounding to the rack against the mirrored wall.

He grabs a dumbbell, turns, and makes exaggerated concentration faces at himself as he hoists.

Nobody uses this place except for Josh. It was a selling point of the building when they bought the apartment, but this complex is all young families and elderly people, none of them with the time or energy to be vain. My father doesn't live here anymore, but when he visits it feels like nothing has changed. Outside, in the pool, a gaggle of old women go through their water calisthenics, making soft splashes as their elbows sink and rise.

Josh invited him solely for this. *Watch me work* is how he put it, so my father is watching. He feels his own stomach as he watches Josh's sinews twist. The fat on his belly feels like an overambitious cake collapsing on itself. He sucks in. Josh notices and smiles.

For a moment, my father sees a better version of himself in Josh's face, definitely in his body, the angled lines from his shoulders into his waist. His own father was an obese cab driver with a gambling addiction. My father is not obese, nor is he a gambling addict, nor is he a cab driver, and each of those small victories has led to a generational progression of manhood. He looks at his son, groaning in the name of progress, and tries to focus on that word.

"Let's take a walk," he says. "Come on. Let's go somewhere. Do you want lunch? I'll buy you lunch."

He wants to put this moment on display. He wants people to see them together, wants to feel strangers' eyes trained on his son as all the pistons under his skin pump with each step he takes. Josh will be admired and then my father will think, *I made that, that is a part of me,* and Josh will feel his pride.

"I'm not hungry," Josh says.

"Well then a soda, shit. Or just for a walk. I want to go for a walk with you, is that a crime?"

"I'm not done," Josh says. "Look at the sheet; I'm not close to done."

"Come on, take a half day."

"*No.*"

His voice cracks, mostly because he's seventeen, but there's panic to it as well.

He says, "I don't want to go anywhere, okay?"

"Okay, fine, okay," my father says.

Outside, the old ladies have grabbed paddleboards and are kicking themselves through the pool. They sound like a dishwasher. Josh goes back to his routine. My father goes back to watching, but now he is unsettled. He looks at Josh's fists balled, knuckle-bones ready to poke out of his skin, supporting fifty pounds of metal in each hand. He wonders how many hours a day Josh spends in here, alone, straining. He remembers strain on Josh's face from a decade ago, the throbbing frustration as he tried to explain what he was feeling, what he saw and why it frightened him. It has always hurt my father to see his son strain.

Josh begins to walk toward him, dumbbells still in his hands. He walks until they're only two feet apart, and the dumbbells swing a little in the space between them. My father feels his body tense. He tries to force a chuckle out.

"Muscle beach over here," he says.

"How big you think I can get?" Josh asks.

Was that rhetorical?

"You look great," my father says. And then, "You know, you always did. Look great, I mean. And now, perfect."

He gives a thumbs-up, which hangs benign between their chests.

Josh takes a step closer, and my father's thumb touches the valley between muscles.

Josh's face is running. There's orangey makeup from his hairline to his chin, like a plastic mold, and now, as he sweats, seams are beginning to form. Beads run down his forehead, around his nose, along his cheeks, and they're like zippers opening, revealing actual skin beneath.

My father likes reasons. Everything he has ever done has been for a reason. Everything everybody does should be in service of an end. So how can he not wonder what his son's performance of self is for? Why lift weights to admire the final product alone? Why wear makeup for a workout in front of your dad, just to sweat it off and reapply before bed, leaving smudged, eyeless prints of your face on your pillowcases? Why pump yourself up for a choreographed face-off with a father who never hit you, who wouldn't even know how to do that?

My father sees Josh as a boy again, his *glimpses.* He remembers standing in the bedroom doorway, paralyzed, watching Beth on her knees yelling, *Tell me what you want.*

He was a literature scholar, or trying to be, when Josh was born. He quit that and took a mailroom job because there are basic responsibilities in a productive life that go unspoken. He came home from work and read next to the crib while Josh slept. He was going to someday write a dissertation on Melville because he liked that Melville was a city clerk *and* a genius.

He's thinking of a line from *Moby-Dick* now: *It is the easiest thing in the world for a man to look as if he had a great secret in him.*

That's a cruel thing to think when watching his son.

"You look great," my father says again. "Great."

Outside, the old ladies hoist themselves from the pool and shuffle to the elevator. Josh breaks whatever stare-down has been happening and moves to put the dumbbells away. Then he begins a set of crunches, face disappearing between his knees, reappearing, disappearing again until he's a blur.

There's a beautiful Puerto Rican girl who loves him for a while. The first time my father sees them together, it's his proudest parental moment since he watched Josh play the timpani in a high school orchestra concert. He had been so on beat then. There was the beat, and there was Josh, right on it. Steady, which is always a nice word to think.

This Puerto Rican girl is more of a guitar solo. My father can't remember her name, but names don't seem so important, because she's standing there, hoisted up on thin heels, and Josh is asking her to pirouette. She's doing it for him. She's not happy about it, but she's not unhappy. She is smiling, at least, a wry smile. The heels make her leg muscles tighten, and my father watches the tightening.

She's really hot. Objectively. And charming, at ease with herself in any conversation, the kind of person everyone wants to know. And she's leaning her weight on Josh, certain that he won't let her fall. And he doesn't. And Puerto Rican girls have *options,* mind you, options like big Puerto Rican men who know how to fight and fix engines. And still she chose Josh, she is here smiling next to him. My father can't believe he's thinking this way.

The girl is saying, "It is *so* nice to meet you. I've been so *curious.*"

Josh is smiling broadly, and he appears happy without any complication. My father wishes he could freeze the easy quiet on his son's face. He wants to take them out while it's like this.

He announces that it's dinnertime and puts his hands on the middle of each of their backs, steers them to the door. They have sushi at a fancy place on University and the girl says, "No, this is too much," when she sees the menu, but my father puts his hand on hers from across the table and says, "I *want* to," the words intoxicating as he speaks them.

They stay for hours. Instincts never before triggered rise up in my father, and he tells stories about Josh's cheeks as a baby, and that one time in right field in Little League, and the poem he wrote in middle school, and watching him play the timpani in the orchestra. My father and Josh laugh at the same moments in the stories, and then the girl sees them laugh so she laughs, too, and my father points at her, says to Josh, "A sense of humor. Very nice, very nice."

They drink sake and her face gets flushed. Josh puts the back of his hand on her cheek and she closes her eyes. My father looks out the window and sees the sidewalk crowded, sees passing faces glancing in at him, on the inside, with his son and a girl whose name he can't remember but whose eyes are closed because she's in love. On the street after dinner, everyone is drunk and they hug in a pack of three, elbows like the points of a star.

She disappears quickly and Josh never says why. He never mentions that she existed, and so my father begins to doubt every part of his sushi dinner memory. Josh brings more women to his apartment, every month or so it feels like. He displays each one so that my father may see them. But that feeling from the first time is gone.

It's never a white girl. And that's fine, it's whatever, but now it's only Indian women with names that Josh can perfectly pronounce, that my father doesn't even attempt to repeat. Josh speaks enough Hindi to impress them, which used to also impress my father but now makes him confused and uneasy. The women speak English with accents. Sometimes they speak so quietly that Josh repeats everything they say to make sure it's heard. Then they go silent and sit at the edge of the couch while he talks.

The things that he says.

She's quiet, but you'd be surprised. Tell him, babe, don't be shy. Tell him what you do for me.

My father asks him to stop, but he says it low, drained of conviction, and he is ignored.

They sit for too long. Sometimes the girls try to tell my father,

It's so nice to meet you. I really care about your son. Then my father tries to smile and thank them. One time, the girl gets up to go to the bathroom. When she leaves the room, Josh leans forward at my father and says, "Isn't it great?"

"What?" my father says.

"These girls," Josh says. "You know I can say anything to them. You see that?"

"That is not—" my father begins, stops, begins again. "That is not nice."

There is no weaker thing he could have said. Josh chuckles to himself. My father wants to tell him that he didn't raise him to be like this, but he's not sure if that's true and he doesn't want to risk hearing Josh call *bullshit*.

The toilet flushes and my father snaps back in his seat. He puts his hands on his lap as though he has been caught complicit. Josh laughs again.

The girl is smoothing her skirt as she returns. She smiles.

"Thank you," she says. "But I've got to go now. I'm supposed to meet my sister uptown."

"Stay for a while," Josh says. "Stay for me."

She sits down next to him and says only for a minute. Josh wraps his arm around her neck and pulls her close to him. She smiles at that. She nestles into his chest. His biceps tightens as he runs his fingers through the black hair that hides her face. He's flexing. My father tries to see how much she seems to like the way Josh touches. He tries to focus only on that.

A year later, Josh is still flexing but this time father and son are alone. My father's fingers are on Josh's skin, tracing the raised outline of his new Iron Cross tattoo.

"Is it supposed to be bumpy?" he says. "Are you sure it's not infected?"

"It's not infected."

There isn't much else to say. They're in Josh's apartment that he still doesn't pay rent on because he doesn't have a job. He's a musician who doesn't perform, a writer who doesn't finish, the owner of a business that doesn't turn a profit, and yet he has found enough money to pay for what looks to be a very professionally done tattoo, and who knows how much extra tattoo artists charge for Holocaust symbols.

"It's a mark of strength," Josh says.

This is a test. You don't have to be Freud to realize that a Jewish son showing his father a Nazi tattoo is looking for a reaction.

"Did it hurt?" my father asks, so as not to ask anything else.

"Yeah," Josh says. "Especially when they filled it in. To get all that black filled in, it's like they're running a knife back and forth on your skin in the same spot."

The snake, that fucking snake, slithers by my father's ankle, and he makes a sound like a man on a ledge in a cartoon, waving his arms to not fall. Josh grins and the snake slithers on.

"The idea is that you control the pain," Josh says. "You say, *I am in control of this pain.*"

My father breathes deeply and forces his breath not to quiver because quivering is something Josh would very much want in this moment.

He says, "I guess it doesn't make sense to me. That's all. You're *Jewish.* I have your Bar Mitzvah picture up at home. You're playing the drums."

That last sentence hangs in the air between them, and my father wants, he thinks, only acknowledgment from his son— *I remember what you're talking about, and yes, that version of me did exist.* Josh doesn't say anything, so my father loses control and snarls, "Say something, please."

Josh sighs and takes on a bored teacher's voice. He says, "But why should you care what people will say? All you have to do is please yourself."

"What the fuck are you talking about?"

"Ayn Rand."

"You're quoting *Ayn Rand* to me?"

"It is so fucking typical that you would say it like that. You are so fucking afraid of my self-reliance because that would be such a threat to the Jew landlord."

My father feels his torso snap back, exactly what he hadn't wanted to have happen. Because, again, what does Jewish anti-Semitism want more than to shock somebody? And my father is *not* shocked. That's the point. All this posturing is annoying, fine, it's upsetting, but it's not like his delicate sensibilities have been offended or anything.

"You depend on other people's need," Josh finishes. "That's all I'm saying."

My father really wishes he could go to Melville here: *It is better to fail in originality than to succeed in imitation.* It's the kind of retort that people remember on the way out of a room or later, falling asleep, and he has it *now*, ready to say, and it would be so mean and so true. But that's the problem with a son: You make him see that he is pathetic, and then what? He is your pathetic creation and the whole conversation becomes about blame.

And then there's the nasty reality that my father wouldn't mind at all if Josh succeeded at imitation. This apartment is an attempt at imitation—*Live in it; pretend that it's yours.* Even with the tattoo, my father is reaching for some sense of normalcy in his mind. Josh placed it high on his arm, not on his hand or neck, so it can be covered up for any job interview or family function. He is clinging to that tiniest compromise.

My father sees himself in a moment long buried. He's in the apartment in Sheepshead Bay, holding Josh while he cries and shakes. Josh is looking past him at something that isn't there. My father is saying, *You are my son, Joshua. This is your home. We are in Brooklyn. I am your father and I love you.* He is squeezing Josh, trying to make sure every part of his son's body feels him so that he knows he's anchored to something. Usually my father tries to blink away memories like this, all that vulnerability. But the moments existed, and he wants to be back in them now. He wishes he could still fit his arms easily around his son's torso, wonders what he looks like as he finally falls asleep.

I see you, he thinks. *I have always seen you.*

You have nightmares when you are awake, little boy.

You are smart and scared. You have big, soft eyes that ask for help when you don't want them to.

My father says none of these things, and Josh walks over to the sink. He pours himself some water, chugs it, says that most people don't realize how crucial hydration is to a fully functioning body. Then he says, "Tell me another group throughout history that knew what they wanted and went after it like these guys." He touches the tattoo. "Seriously, tell me."

The snake moves along the counter behind him, making a sound like a whisper. Josh keeps fast-talking about discipline and purity, how if you put the politics aside, what's wrong with the idea of purity as a goal?

My father doesn't want to argue. He opts for humor instead.

"Jesus Christ, it's going to be awkward at Passover this year," he says.

Josh laughs and that makes my father laugh because Josh sounds the way he has always sounded laughing and my father never thinks about how much he loves that sound until he hears it. They are comfortable with laughter. They both understand it and let it linger, a truce.

They don't speak for a long time. Or, if they do, none of the speaking made it to my father's memory, which has streamlined, looking for major plot points and at least semi-plausible symbolism. Their relationship picks up again when Beth calls.

My father answers and she says, "Your son just came home. He was in rehab at Beth Israel. Did you know?"

She says it without any emotion; she's just reporting the latest. My father answers, "Oh," and then says, "I'll come over," to which Beth does not protest, so he goes to get his jacket.

He walks to the F-train at West Fourth and plans emotions to express, but he doesn't feel any of those emotions. He walks downstairs to the tracks. He remembers riding the subway with Josh and holding his hand. He remembers the acute awareness of how close the third rail was, remembers putting his body in between his son and the danger. He remembers Josh at his legs watching strangers pass in train cars, watching his own face reflected and blurred in each window.

At the end of the platform, a withered man, chalky pale with matted white hair running from his chest up his neck to his face, plays Neil Young on an acoustic guitar. It's "The Needle and the Damage Done." He sings that line about junkies being like setting suns and his voice catches. My father thinks that this must be a hallucination. He puts five dollars in the man's coffee cup and the man is real. The man looks up and says thank you with the flat tone of someone who is always thanking and never has cause to be thanked. He closes his eyes and sings on.

Josh is on the balcony at Beth's apartment, looking out at the East River.

My father takes a breath like he's about to go underwater, then walks up and puts his hand on his son's shoulder.

"Why'd you do that?" he says.

Josh looks up. He snarls. His face is feral.

"I'm a bad guy, Dad," he says.

What does that kind of shit even mean?

"You want to be a junkie for your life?" my father says.

The correct answer is no. Josh says nothing. My father begins to say something nagging, but Josh interrupts him.

"I want to be a thief," he says. "I want to be a criminal."

They watch the river together. A ferry full of tourists ambles through the water. My father sees a flashbulb go off.

There is no more beautiful place in the world than New York from a distance, when you can't make out any people and when you can't hear any noise, but there it is, rising out of the water, stacks of gold light outlined by dusk. Everything else is disappointment.

"What?" Josh says, chiding.

"Nothing."

"I'm a bad guy," he says again.

When he first bought this place, my father would bring Josh out on the balcony. Josh would look down and get scared, and my father would tell him don't look down, look out. They would watch the skyline and try to imagine everything they couldn't see: Who lives there? Who is standing on that roof right now? What are they doing?

My father isn't sure if this is a memory or a wish.

He wants to ask his son for a lot of details, but he doesn't ask anything.

"You're not bad," he says, and Josh sneers.

They are telling two different stories about two different men and maybe neither one exists, but they don't care. This is the conversation that will happen too often from now on. Once you have this conversation, it feels like the only conversation to have.

I am bad.

No, you're not. You're good, I swear, I see it.

Until those are the only two options.

My father leaves.

He retraces his steps to the subway, rides back to Manhattan. A homeless couple sits across from him and they slump into each other. He breathes through his mouth and doesn't look at them. He has always been quick to look away. Smells make him retch easily. If alone, he has to sleep with all the lights on.

When he was a boy, his mother wouldn't let him in the house while she cleaned. She tied string around a paper bag holding his lunch and dangled it down for him. He smiles at that memory, the routine. He whistles to himself, wet and tuneless. That's what he does when there is something he'd rather not say or see. He never noticed it until Josh began making fun of him on a beach, one summer. He started whistling in the middle of conversations and everyone would laugh. Then, for years, Josh would say something ridiculous and my father would ask, *What?* Or, *Why?* And Josh would say, "I'm just trying to make you whistle."

When was that?

Where was that?

The junkie with the guitar is gone from the station when my father exits, and there is no more music. He wonders where a man like that goes when he's done playing his song.

My father came to me today from West Fourth, and soon he will ride back there, but now he's in my kitchen eyeing the roach motels I have lining the walls. He's complaining about the Internet.

"So many websites," he says.

"What?" I say.

"I mean, the problem with the Internet," he says, "is that everybody has a story that they feel like you should be reading, and they're all there, so you read them."

He's still sweating from the tennis. He smells the way he always smells when he sweats. He isn't looking at me, but past me, out the window at the brick wall of the building across the alley.

"I used to read all the literature on all these rehab websites," he says. "That's what I did that first night I found out, after I got home from the train. I just kept doing it. I hated all of it. I thought all the stories and all the promises were so stupid, you know? But then I read more."

I like this idea, the effort he made to understand in the best way he knew how.

"Did you know Boz Scaggs had a son who overdosed?" he says.

"Who's Boz Scaggs?" I say.

"Are you serious?"

He tries to hum a Boz Scaggs song, wet and tuneless, then stops.

He says, "Boz Scaggs wrote this thing after his son died, and he called him *fine, beautiful, sweet.* I remember that. This was maybe a year before Josh died, and I remember thinking, if somebody asked me, what words would I use?"

Mostly, he just looked for rehab centers and survivors who swore they knew something that nobody else had figured out yet.

How often?

"Every night," he tells me, like it's really important that I believe that detail.

He would lie next to my mother and wait until she fell asleep, and then he would slide down the hall to the computer, not wanting to lift his feet and put them down again on creaking wood. He would look into the screen and feel the blue light stinging his eyes. He would see himself reflected in the window, pale from the light, and old. He would let the platitudes wash over him.

Are you losing somebody you love? Find them again.

We are offering a 92% success rate!

Recover your sense of spiritual meaning, purpose, belonging, and personal fulfillment.

Allow God to rid your life of addiction's grasp.

"All of that bullshit," my father says. He gives a dismissive wave.

The issue, I think, is the assumption that logic can be imposed on the illogical. He was supposed to buy that basic, flawed concept. That a story with a complete narrative could be made out of needles in arms, decisions that become no longer decisions, sickness. That it was a matter of strategy and will.

"Josh believed," my father says. "He would tell me, *Now* I know what I need to do. He would talk to me about self-reliance and transformation. It was the same shit I was reading every night, like he read it, too, and internalized it. He'd say, Trust me, this is working, why do you worry like that? *Why do I worry?*"

My father is angry at someone who no longer exists. He's asking a rhetorical question of a man who is in no position to answer it. Josh promised him until the end that the end wasn't coming, and then the end came and he never had to acknowledge how ridiculous it was, all those things he expected his father to believe.

He wants to know if I see that. The end was inevitable, certainly from the time when he stood with Josh on the balcony on Roosevelt Island, probably from before then. Something was set in motion, something in the marrow of how his son was, not bad, not undeserving, just cracked. When you tell the story of an addict, it's so easy for everything to become about potential triumph, and triumph implies change and change implies a choice.

"I believed that he was trying," my father says. "But that was never the point."

Now I see Josh's face, as clear as any memory of him I've ever had. He's in this cramped kitchen of mine next to the fridge covered in party Polaroids. He's the size that he really was, which is to say pretty average, but he's older in this memory so he's fat. He is looking at me and our father. He is waving.

This is a very specific memory, the way he looked at both of us together, the way he waved with a heavy right hand, held it by his ear and then dropped it quickly. He's smiling and his eyes are narrowed into pinched crescents. His face is racked. He is holding it so tight, and his skin doesn't move from that wide smile because he's forcing it to stay. This strain is not something I've ever remembered on his face. I want to place the memory, but I can't yet.

"I used to sit in his apartment the way I'm sitting in yours now," my father says. "Remember that big captain-of-industry desk he had? He would sit behind it and try to tell me all the things he was going to do. He always did that, even before he was using. He had all these pads of paper in the desk drawers, and these nice pens. He would pitch me ideas—movies, novels, businesses. You know what he told me one time? He was sitting behind that silly fucking desk, and he said, Dad, right now, if I got my body back to where it was, if I practiced, I could be a Major League Baseball player. I could be anything. I really believe that."

He looks at me and begins to laugh, then stops. He leans back in his chair and raises both hands, palms up.

"Isn't that what you want someone to think?" I ask softly.

"I wanted him to make *sense*," my father says. His voice catches.

I remember where the memory is from. It's from the last time I saw Josh, a sunny afternoon a couple of weeks, maybe, before he died.

The scene begins in Sima's memory, a moment with him that she described to me that I have stolen and blown up in my imagination.

They were in a café, talking. Josh had been clean for nearly a month, which had happened a few times since she'd known him, but he said this time was different, something about how unfiltered the sunlight felt, the warmth of spring air. He'd been staying at Beth's, sleeping in his childhood twin bed. He was letting his mother be kind to him, he swore it. He let her bring him soup during the night shivers, let her sit outside the door and ask him if he was okay, as he lay in a lukewarm bath because the water didn't sting as much as the air. Finally, the air stopped stinging.

Josh was trying to tell Sima just how *vivid* the world was when withdrawal stopped. He described it like lying under one of those lead X-ray blankets and then feeling the technician take it off, so for a moment you're nearly floating.

"Look at my eyes," he told her. She did; they were clear. They both smiled.

Their coffees were empty and she had to leave. When she stood up, he grabbed her hand and said, "The next time you see me, I will still look like this. I want to take you to dinner. I know the place already. You'll love it."

They hugged good-bye and he squeezed her and she smelled him.

He walked downtown. I imagine his walk.

He passed Fourteenth Street, that corner with all the card tables displaying bootlegged DVDs. Like always, the DVD men whispered to him: *Smoke? Snort? Shoot?* He moved on, eyes at his shoelaces. He passed the basketball court at West Fourth Street and again, from men leaning against trees, standing shadowed on the top step of the subway entrance: *Smoke? Snort? Shoot?*

Josh told himself a story: I am not that man.

I opened the front door and he was standing there. My father made a startled sound behind me. We hadn't seen Josh for a while. I wanted to ask how long he'd been standing there debating whether to ring the doorbell, but I didn't.

"Hi," he said. "Is this a bad time?"

My father and I were holding baseball gloves and heading to an asphalt park down the street. My father told him he could come with us, he could watch if he wanted, and he said, "I'd like that."

I remember that I hugged Josh, but then he fell back, walked a step or two behind us on the narrow sidewalk. I remember now, more than I recognized it then, that my father didn't turn around to him, kept his neck stiff as we crossed Sixth Avenue. When I turned around, Josh's eyes were on the back of my father's head, and his lips were moving around words.

They stood next to each other, facing me, as my father and I threw. Josh leaned into my father's ear and spoke. I think he was telling him what he told Sima—*I am clean, I have been clean, look at my eyes, the next time you see me they'll be exactly the same.* My father smiled, resisted looking, threw. I threw back as hard as I could, wanting to impress.

We walked home together from the park, and Josh draped a heavy arm over my shoulders. I stiffened, then slackened.

"You look good," I said.

"I am," he said.

"You do look good," my father said.

"I am," he said.

He stood on the stoop when we got home, and I had the realization that all three of us were trying to picture the act of him walking inside.

My father and I stood above him.

My father said, "Well."

Josh said, "Well."

When we were about to go in, Josh said, "I'll be back soon. I'll call ahead next time. The three of us can have dinner. Maybe next week?"

I didn't know if I believed him, and I heard that uncertainty in my voice when I said, "Yeah, sounds good."

That's when he looked up at us, raised his right hand to wave good-bye, held it by his ear, and then dropped it to his side. His eyes were pinched crescents, and he was trying very hard to keep smiling. I think he wanted to say more, but then the door closed.

It's what happened next that my father can't stop thinking about because it's what he can't know.

Josh went back to Beth's after he left us, and at some point in the next week or so he told her that he was ready to be alone, that he could be trusted to be alone. He returned to his apartment, all the faded black leather, the pull-up bar so long unused, his keyboard dusty, his notebooks stacked under the coffee table.

I don't know if the hit that killed him was already in his apartment, a last stash that he hadn't been able to bring himself to flush, or if he got antsy in there alone and went down to Tompkins Square Park to buy from the gutter punks, or if he called a dealer to deliver and there was a stranger who sat with him at the end, impossible now to find. What I do know is that the only piece of writing or correspondence left in Josh's apartment dated within a month of his death was the warning letter from the Supreme Court of New York: *YOU ARE HEREBY ORDERED to appear for a VIOLATION OF PROBATION HEARING.* The one that I found in a torn-up shopping bag on top of a pile of crinkled loose-leaf love letters.

I ask my father what Josh was arrested for. He doesn't know. When? No answer. We speculate about what he might have done. He got kicked out of a methadone program once; did he try to buy it illegally? Or was he selling it? It could have been an old prescription forgery charge. Or credit card fraud; he was good at fraud. A prostitution sting. That's definitely possible, my father says. These are the options that we hope for because they make, at least, a small bit of sense.

"I don't know what he might have done," my father says. "Whatever he really did, the full extent of it, he didn't want me to know."

I'm not sure that the original crime matters. What matters is that on the day he died this might well have been the last piece of evidence he saw to tell him the story of who he was. And the voice, official, threatening, inarguable, said, *You are a case number. You have done wrong and you have not atoned, but you will.*

I see Josh fold the letter back into itself, put it in the shopping bag on top of all the other voices, the kind ones, the ones that spoke of the good in him. And that's when the last change of mind enters the scene, and the drug, and the desire to feel outside himself. It's the best approximation I've found to speculate about, anyway. Who was he at the end? What was he seeing? What was he thinking? Maybe he was thinking that there was no story to tell anymore beyond the official one.

A few days later, Beth called my father because Josh wasn't picking up the phone. He met her outside the apartment. Neither spoke; both knew and weren't sure how.

My father opened the door with the spare key. The window was open, and he could hear rain falling on the hardwood floor. He wondered if they should hold hands, him and Beth, like kids in the summer before they jump off rocks into the water. My father never learned how to swim.

There was a tiny staircase, three steps was all, that led from the kitchen into the living room of the apartment. They descended and saw Josh lying by the coffee table. He was in his underwear, white briefs. The elastic cut into his waist. Next to him was a bottle of Formula 409 cleaning spray and a sponge. It had always made him feel relief to clean. My father remembered that and almost smiled.

Beth trembled and held back. My father did what was grotesque and somehow right, paternal at least. He knelt and touched two fingers to his son's flesh. It was cold, so that was it.

The police came. There was an official report. He rode the ambulance to the morgue. There was a death certificate. He went home.

"I'm not saying that would make it a suicide," my father says, so many years past that night, still reaching. "But, you know, it's a reason. If he saw that summons and it was the last straw . . ."

There is a morsel of redemption in the notion of a man attempting to rewrite what he is one last time, then coming home, seeing something that can't be changed, deciding to finally close his eyes and stop trying. I'd like to think of him feeling resigned rather than desperate, still guilty and flailing to the very end. But then there's the Formula 409 and the sponge, the implied promise to himself of a new shine when he woke up.

I try not to think about that detail, the broad symbolism that it might hold. Instead, I try to imagine his last thoughts because there's potential in that.

I still have the one book he ever gave me, Rand's *Anthem*. It was a birthday present. He handed it to me and told me not to let the world hold me back. I hope he didn't remember Ayn Rand platitudes as he nodded away.

There's a Baldwin line that says it best, another from "Sonny's Blues": *It ain't only the bad ones, nor yet the dumb ones that get sucked under.*

I hope he was thinking something like that as he faded, on the scuffed wood floor looking at his ceiling, hearing voices from out on Twenty-Sixth Street like he wasn't alone.

I'm at my parents' place now, under the wall of Josh's beforeshots. Across from me, my father leans back in his chair and can't figure out when he believed, when he stopped believing. Did he worry the whole time? Did he know? Was it as inevitable as it seems now? Did anything change at all?

The addiction clouds things. Scenes condense and then they begin to eat their own edges.

The story of addiction is the story of memory, and how we never get it right.

We're still having this conversation.

We're sitting in front of the TV and it's another Sunday.

"When I think back, it's mostly about the death," my father tells me. "I talk to him sometimes. I yell. *You fucking idiot.* That kind of stuff. I think about things disappearing. His face eroding until it's gone."

He goes silent after that. He slurps tea and I sip beer, and on the TV in the background men are hitting each other and whistles are blowing. When I leave, he looks like he wants to say something else, but he doesn't.

I get an email from him changing his story again. He remembers Josh's smile, he says, and calls it shy. Josh just wanted to feel better, he says, and why shouldn't he want that? We all want that. He had a shy smile and he wanted to feel better. My father remembers Josh near the end, telling him he understood how hard it was to see him—a conscious gift of acknowledgment, one meant to heal.

Maybe I'm just trying to put a gloss on it, my father says.

[NOTEBOOK, JUNE 16, 1995, "NOTES"]:

And to think, I myself wonder at times why I suck on the sap. As they all torment me. Torment. I won't let the torment in. The red juice even tastes good now.

[POEM, JUNE 18, 1995, "FATHER'S DAY"]:

Absolution from the sap.
In the sap, it destroys

All that irks me.
All the people that desert me.
And it takes me,
Yes it makes me,
At one with all.
And if the terror, or horror, or ugliness
Calls
It is washed away
In a sea of red,
The sweet, slow rocking of my head.
When you see me I'll be fixed.
For I was broken.
I was sick.
The sea of red and what it brought.
One day soon I will be king.
I'll shout, rooftops,
Much I will say.
How my cares were killed on father's day.

He writes nothing else until Labor Day, and I yearn to see that summer. It's the closest thing I can find to a beginning of his addiction, that bizarrely reassuring *change* moment, when his original self and his addict self can be last separated. He entered a young man in pain, a young man searching. The red sap rocked him sweetly, slowly, and how necessary that must have felt, to be rocked. The sap was prescription cough syrup; I'm pretty sure. By Labor Day, he's submerged.

I imagine joy in the four months of no writing between these entries. I imagine that he recorded no promises, no vengeance notes, no sad poems, no posturing scripts, because there was no reason to. He was not detached from the sensation of being himself; he was reveling in it instead. There's nothing to say about happiness; you just live it. That's a cliché, yes, but I hope that it's a true one. He felt joy. From Father's Day on, for a whole summer, his cares were killed. He left no evidence, he just felt it. After all this looking, maybe the best explanation is in the silence.

On Labor Day, his writing is shaky and smudged. He's high, but the joy is gone:

[NOTEBOOK, SEPTEMBER 4, 1995, "LABOR AND ABSOLUTION FOR A JUNKIE"]:

Most of my life was bad. Awful. But the third day of a three day weekend was always the worst. The success and the horror are what I need to write about. How to go from horror to neutral and from neutral to good. The red, sweet sap elevated me to good. But I have a great task before me. Life. And I feel overwhelmed. I blame the sap, but that's not the reason.

It's illegible after this. There is no reason given, no confession, nothing easy. Just the stories we tell ourselves, and now we're back to the beginning. Now we try again. In his email to me, my father is already trying again. When Josh died, it was rock bottom, he says. And if he'd lived, he would have shown his goodness more, his softness. There wouldn't have been anger; there wouldn't have been shame. I think I believe that, my father says.

· · ·

Time passes.

Time has been passing, and he has been fading, and I have been making phone calls, meeting for coffee, writing, deleting, turning yellowed pages covered in blue ink.

I've moved. From Brooklyn out to the Midwest, back East again to an old industrial city where none of my family has ever been. I have a hard-bodied leather suitcase, and that's where I keep Josh's writing. I've taken the suitcase with me wherever

I've lived, and many nights, always alone, I've opened it and read.

Sofia and I are getting married soon, at a quaint New England inn with white walls. Dave is going to be my best man. I proposed on a hiking trail in the Midwest, kneeling on a damp carpet of fall leaves. Our dog ran around our legs. That's another thing I did, bought a dog. She is harmless and adorable and falls asleep on my belly sometimes.

In the old industrial city back East, I wake up early and take her to shit on a little dirt patch by the edge of a parking lot on the corner. I'm spacing out, and I look down to see her nosing a hypodermic needle that's been javelined into the dirt. There are fresh blood flecks around it. I pull the dog off and hear a motor running. A few feet away, someone parked for the night to get high. The window is cracked just enough so they don't suffocate; the heat is on so they don't freeze to death.

These are the small moments that still mean too much to me, that I have a hard time walking away from quickly. I stand over the car, staring through the cracked window. It's a boy, younger than me. His seat is reclined as far back as possible. At first I can't see him breathing and I don't know what to do, but then his chest moves, just a little, up and down, and then again. Then he shivers in his sleep. I put my hand on the roof of the car and lean closer. He looks ordinary. Everything about this is ordinary.

It's the commonness that's most wrenching.

This is a good parking lot to get high in; they never tow. When this boy wakes, he will drive away and do this again somewhere else because that's what he does, that's what a lot of people do. Eventually, I assume, he won't wake up. I have this urge to tell him, *Hey, I knew someone who didn't wake up.* Not as a warning or anything, but because maybe he would be interested.

The dog is cold and has finished shitting, so she barks at me. The boy begins to wake. I leave quickly, tugging the leash down the block to my apartment, where it's warm and Sofia is sleeping, curled like an infant, breathing long and full. At home, too, are Josh's journals, hiding under a stack of old comforters in a hallway closet, which is where I always return them after reading, as though my interest is definitively done each time. They're tucked away with my boxing gloves left over from a brief fitness craze and Sofia's plastic, portable Christmas tree.

Toward the end, in his second-to-last notebook, Josh began a memoir. He called it a "true novel." It is ten handwritten pages and ends mid-sentence. There's a faded pen line running down from the last letter to the end of the page.

[NOTEBOOK, UNDATED, "THE JUNKIE AND THE VISITOR: A TRUE NOVEL," P. 1]:
Now, I'm not one to say, "Yo, I'm from the streets, G." Mostly because that isn't me. I'm a rich man's son. But the streets are open to anyone. Be warned.

This is written as an annotation, scribbled in a box on the top of the page and linked to the rest of the text by an arrow, amending all the story that is to come. It's an honest assessment.

The memoir pushes on. It's just one scene with two characters: our narrator, nameless, and a man named Andy, who, though not telling the story, is the protagonist. Andy brings the drug over. Andy wants to freebase. Andy has had a bad day. The narrator does it to appease Andy, calls himself altruistic. And even when he agrees to get high on a day when he hadn't been planning to, we never see the narrator taking a hit and we never feel his sensation. We just watch Andy, our Gatsby, experiencing pain and joy, then almost death.

[NOTEBOOK, UNDATED, "THE JUNKIE AND THE VISITOR: A TRUE
NOVEL," PP. 9–10]:

*The small, white rock looked like candy and was placed into the
tin foil holder that Andy had shaped like a taco. He took an old,
empty, hollow blue pen and placed it strategically over the white
rock. He lit his flame under it, and all at once a sizzle sound was
made and the white stone shrunk. Then the smoke came up. And
up. And up. Andy was determined to get every last molecule of that
gas. No smoke could escape Andy's ambition. He kept the flame
going. I mean there was enough for three or four good-sized hits.
But Andy is a junkie. The only amount that is ever enough is the
whole amount and that's never enough either.*

*When the last wisp of smoke came up and he sucked it down,
he collapsed. Not so much from the effects of the drug, but
because he hadn't let himself have oxygen for a minute or so.
So he lay supine on the floor. I thought I could feel the electric
currents running through him. I didn't know what to do. Maybe
he just wanted to lie there until he needed his next hit.*

"Yo, Andy," I said.

*Andy jumped up like a jackrabbit, like nothing had even
happened.*

"Family!" he said.

This is where the pen runs down the page and whatever idea
was there is lost. I have looked for more of Andy or his like, some
other mention of friends who lived with my brother high, in
the moments that he kept from the rest of us. There is nothing.
Other than this abandoned scene, Josh writes almost exclusively
of hard, unfair pasts and certain, triumphant futures. Being high
rarely made him want to tell the story of being high. Instead, it
made all the other stories better—hardships harder, triumphs
more triumphant.

I wonder if Andy was fictive, or not exactly fictive but a part of Josh, the swashbuckling and brave addict he wanted to be. The one who is resurrected before the scene even has a chance to get frightening.

The more I read from him, the more I rehash the stories he told other people, the more my brother becomes fiction altogether. More than a decade after he died, his pages spread out in front of me and he is still hiding. Look at Andy, he says. Andy is a junkie. See him use, but don't look at me.

When I visit New York, Dave and I walk around the block to get high, nothing serious, just stubby joints filled with dry, browned weed. We leave our father, who glowers but doesn't say anything. We stand in a dark doorway, hidden as best we can be from accusing streetlights, and we act like teenagers. It's windy. I cup my hands around the joint. Dave holds it in his mouth and lights it. The sputtering flame glows across his face, shadows churning like an ocean up his cheeks to his eyes. His eyes are Josh's eyes, a flecked, layered brown. Or maybe they're not.

Dave is okay in that he's sharp, functioning, and the only drug he uses habitually is weed. He identifies as an addict. He went to a rehab facility outside Scranton for a week, but he was surrounded, he says, by a group of alcoholic firefighters and the place became this macho redemption contest. He says that most people who think, for sure, that they're *quitting,* have *quit,* are insufferable. He went to meetings for a while and my father went with him, but then they stopped. I still worry that he's going to die. When I haven't heard from him in a few weeks, I text him something short and stupid, and once he answers I forget to respond.

Dave is on a Cream kick, which makes him seem more stoned than he is.

"Listen to this," he says, holding out his iPod.

I don't want to. I say that. I don't like Cream.

"I don't think you get it," he says.

"I fucking get it," I say. "I just think it's kind of indulgent."

He gives a grimace and then forces one of his earbuds on me. We stand, wire-connected, in a doorway, hiding from light, reeking of bad weed, nodding along to a bluesy jam, and trying to say profound things.

"Listen to Ginger Baker," Dave says. "Listen to the *drums*."

"Uh-huh," I say.

The drums roll in spasms. Dave rolls his shoulders along with the sound of the drums. I take my earbud out and the music lingers over the sidewalk, faint.

This is an image that recurs in Burroughs's drug writing, surprisingly gentle. Over the gaping needle holes and the ass fucking, music floats in broken streams, brief, invisible. Over and over, when somebody is trying to speak to the narrator, or when he is trying to remember something, the words and the meaning disperse, *like music down a windy street.*

What's that famous story about Burroughs? How he wrote by cutting apart pages and scenes and sentences, refitting newly scissored passages into one another? That's where the repetition comes in—the images that fit everywhere, that mean the most. Music down a windy street. I think it's because of the uncertainty. The sound that is so familiar, but you can't even be sure it's there. It's a junkie's soundtrack, what you want to hear, what you need to believe that you hear.

What can this story be but fragments? Lies? Little packages of what we want to remember, what we want to tell—can you hear it? Faintly? Down this windy street?

"How did Josh play the drums?" I ask Dave. "Who did he play like?"

I remember reading a description of Keith Moon that said he played to the very limits of control, and that's what I want to hear. Dave hunches his shoulders up by his ears like he's cold or embarrassed. Then he starts swinging his arms furiously.

"Josh played like this," he says. "He tried to be so loud that you couldn't hear anyone else. Like he couldn't fully *feel* the music, you know? Listen to the way Ginger *feels* it."

He closes his eyes.

"Sometimes I remember the way it sounded when Josh played," Dave says. "It wasn't bad, it's just . . . when you have to try so hard to make something sound right, it never is."

He has to go. We hug, the kind where two men beat on each other's backs with open palms. He's returning to Beth's apartment on Roosevelt Island, where Josh's room is still intact, door closed. Tonight, he will walk down the hall and he will remember rage and drums played too loud, and if he's feeling generous maybe he will remember the words of a poem.

Beth will watch him from her kitchen, and maybe in his back she will see her other son's, hear Josh's voice through the door when Dave sings in the shower.

In Park Slope, on his couch with his cat, maybe Philip Goodman still hears Josh calling his name—*Phil, Phil, Phil, Phil.* And maybe he finds a way to pity him.

Maybe Lena Milam, tucking her blond girls under a yellow comforter, thinks of unbrushed teeth and tender silence.

Maybe Daniel Chang can still make out Josh's music, echoing and fuzzed, as he trudges through Bed Bath & Beyond looking for hand towels.

Maybe Caleb hears splashing as he tries to sleep, pictures Josh's head bobbing just above the surface of black water, refusing to sink.

And people who are strangers to me, those who disappeared.

Priya, who loved him and saw him leave her—maybe she remembers how she posed and pouted in all the pictures he saved. And the whores who ran out on his worst impulses—how bad is everything that they remember? And the nameless junkie woman in the Astoria apartment—maybe she survived and still feels his body next to hers. And Andy, if Andy still exists or ever did exist, maybe he remembers tying Josh off, nodding at his side. And those he made music with. And those he fucked. And those at the methadone clinics and the meetings, the ones who might have heard the closest thing to honesty.

And Sima at home in Queens. She still hears the way he breathed when they talked. So slow. Did it stop? No, there it was again. She remembers whispering, *Are you there?*, into the phone. *Are you there? Are you there?*

I'm surrounded by other people's memories, other people's eyes. Other people's voices, like a radio that cannot hold a signal, that sounds like every song. His voice is there, too, the softest.

So much is undated, but I think I found Josh's last writing. It's in a marbled notebook that he returned to, off and on, for years. He writes, as usual, of childhood struggles and future glory. Then there's a break. He folds a page into an arrow to separate what comes after. On the next page he writes: *Whenever I put an entry into this notebook, it was under the influence of drugs.* Like it's a sign to disregard.

Then there's another page. He tries to start over, something new, something better. He writes: *Humans, as all animals, are ruled by basic instincts: survival, in all its many facets, and power, in the true Nietzschean sense. In every "animal" group, there is a social pecking order. Outside of this, there is the same thing between different species. Look at lions and zebras and imperialism.*

He stops there and gives up. Another page is folded into an arrow, and on that arrow he tries to start over one last time. He writes: *My Works, #1.* Then the next page, the final one:

Ich bin eine junkie. You know what is so damn ironic? In this very notebook where I

It's another day. I am back in New York alone. I'm leaving the birthday party for somebody who is not my friend but who I kind of know. It's at a karaoke bar somewhere on the far East Side, downtown. It's late and cold. I walk along Delancey Street, the opposite direction of my parents' home, toward the East River. There's a billboard on top of what was once a tenement building, what is now a doorman condo. It's an ad for itself.

I remember when I started all this, I went down to the Harm Reduction Center near Delancey to interview some of the counselors, and this billboard was a *Village Voice* ad. It said "Where Have All the Junkies Gone?" in newspaper-headline font. Because a thriving real estate market and a drastic increase in fusion restaurants don't, or shouldn't, coexist with the scabby, needle-pocked masses who once huddled over subway grates for a burst of warm air. But, of course, that's why this neighborhood is so cool, so moneyed. Who doesn't want proximity to a little danger?

That's what I always wanted from Josh. Or something like that. There's a reason why we tell the addict story so many times that it becomes too easy to anticipate the next turn, the pause for a gasp or a slow head shake. He wanted to be something unlike himself. I wanted that, too, still do, but I don't think I ever had the courage or the desperation, whichever term you like, to give up control. What I remember most, when I remember at all, are the moments when it was just the two of us, and I remember being afraid. I liked that. And he was gentle to me. He was gentle to me, and that felt good, but underneath it was the rush, the fear, the possibility that something big and bad was about to happen.

The East River shudders in the wind. The water wrinkles,

then smoothes. There's a police boat moving toward me, some-where in the black between Manhattan and Brooklyn. Its spot-light is on, scanning the surface of the water like a long white finger pointing to the sky.

I worked at a baseball camp on the river once. I was leading the kids to their morning game, and cops were leaning over the side of the pier, hoisting a bluish arm out of the water. I remem-ber it seemed so impossible that they found the body or that the body found its way back to shore.

In Paris, once, I walked along the Seine with Sofia and every-thing was so beautiful that I felt nervous. In the middle of the river, under a stone bridge, a police boat was stopped and two black-clothed cops pulled a dead man from the water. I think I said something pretentious about how there is so much hidden underneath every perfect thing, and then we held each other.

I walk north until Manhattan juts out. I think I can see the bottom of Roosevelt Island. It's there, hard to distinguish, a few lights in the high-rises still on. I look back at the water.

I remember one more thing, and I haven't remembered it for a long time. Josh and I at my parents' place. It was one of the last weekends he tried to change the story and quit, came over for a safe detox. But he wasn't making promises this time. There was no bluster over the phone. There was only a body, deteriorated, submerged.

Josh lay in the bathtub.

My parents left on a date night. At the door, my mother said, "Honey, are you sure you're okay?"

I said, "Yeah, fine."

My father said, "What's going to happen? He's in the bath."

My mother said, "Just watch TV."

Down the hall from Josh, I watched public-access porn. I tried to imagine classmates' faces on surgically stretched adult bodies.

I tried to imagine the sensation I would feel on my cheeks if they were sandwiched in silicone. I pulled my sweatpants out and inspected, found two new pubic hairs.

There were sounds echoing out from under the bathroom door. I was supposed to ignore them. If the sounds stopped for a while, too long, I was supposed to, well, no, don't worry about it, that's not going to happen. The sounds got louder. I muted the TV so I could hear him, listened to his low moans over the visuals of two fake blondes sucking a double-sided dildo like the spaghetti in *Lady and the Tramp*. Then I turned the TV off. I sat in the dark, listened to my own breath, and listened to him. I thought of movies where pretty, young, white-dude protagonists were tortured but didn't break. I liked those characters. I pictured him as one.

When I heard his voice crack, a pained whinny and then a little gasp, the fantasy stopped. The bathroom door was open and I let myself think this was on purpose. The room smelled of shit and vomit and sweat. I breathed through my mouth. I tiptoed in to stand over him. The water shuddered when he writhed. The water was oily with his grime and the soap that he poured into it. The soap bottle lay on the floor next to him, squeezed empty, as though there was a logical correlation to be found—the more soap, the better the chance to be cleansed. The suds covered him, stuck to his arm hairs, clumped over his crotch. His knees broke through the surface, and I reached out to touch the skin that was available.

His eyes were red. I'm sure they were other things, but all I remember is red, the brightness of it, the idea of it. He focused his gaze on me, and I thought I could see the effort in that.

"Ow," he said and then he smiled, but it turned into a wince. He put his hand on top of mine and it was heavy but I didn't move.

"I'm sorry," I said.

When he breathed, his body heaved. I watched his nipples poke through the water and then disappear again. His submerged skin was nearly translucent. He was perfectly visible but just obscured enough to be a glow, a suggestion, something approximating a human being, the outline and the general shading.

He didn't speak, so I stood to go.

"Stay," he said.

I stayed. I reached out my hand. I wiped the wet strings of hair from his forehead, the way I remembered adult hands doing to me as a feverish child.

He smiled and I asked why and he said, "Nothing." We were quiet again.

He took my hand and put it on his cheek, and I knelt beside him. I let my palm cup his cheekbones, still elegant. He tried to smile again, and there was such softness in it, such fear that I would not smile back. I think I was aware of that, how much he didn't want me to not smile. I felt sadness and I felt love.

"This hurts so much," he said.

I didn't say anything.

"Is this water fucking freezing or what?" he said.

I put my hand in the water and it scalded, so I said no.

"Bullshit," he said.

"Oh, maybe it is," I said.

"No, I'm sorry," he said. "I'm sorry. I'm sorry. I'm sorry." Over and over until it felt like there weren't any spaces between the words.

He didn't tell me a story. There was nobody there to shape the story for him. There was no beginning to this moment, and he spoke of no ending that we would soon reach. He said that it hurt and he said he was sorry.

He let his body slide lower, so just his face poked through

the water. He put his hand on the edge of the tub, kept his fingers wedged between mine. I stayed to be sure he wouldn't let himself sink. I stayed because we were touching. I stayed and watched the pain move in little pulses across his face. I wanted him to feel better than he felt.

Acknowledgments

This book could not have been written without the generosity of a lot of people. It was an act of collaborative memory, and my undying thanks go to every person who spoke with me about Josh, who took time out of their busy lives to dig into difficult memories. Many of the names have been changed, and I will not list them here, but each person brought so much kindness and intelligence to our conversations. You each breathed new life into his story for me. Thank you.

My family, in particular, has been so open and supportive throughout the researching and writing of this book. Writing about family is, in many ways, the repeated poking of an open wound, an enormous and perhaps unfair request to make of those who lived the experiences. I am fortunate to have a family full of smart, caring, supportive readers and writers. To my mother and my father, my brother and his mother: thank you for your uncommon willingness to find value in this project. I am amazed by your generosity, both intellectual and emotional.

Another thing that amazes me: how much it helps to have brilliant, honest writers looking out for you. *Lord Fear* would never have gotten off the ground if it weren't for the tutelage of the great Amitava Kumar. It wouldn't have reached its final form without Ariel Lewiton and Kristen Radtke, who took time away from their own work to help make mine better.

Victoria Marini, my intrepid agent, reader, and friend, has championed this project for so long, with indefatigable patience, even in my brattiest moments. Thank you is not nearly sufficient, but thank you, Victoria, for everything. And thank you also to Keith Goldsmith, my editor, for your steady sage advice, for making this a much tighter book than the one you first encountered. And to Michiko Clark, as well, for embracing this book and working so passionately to publicize it.

Finally, most importantly, I must thank "Sofia," whose real name is much cooler and who has read every word of every draft of *Lord Fear,* including some really terrible early ones, and who I learn from every day. There will never be a satisfactory way to say it: I love you. I love you.